HE LOOKS LIKE ME

An evidence based guide for teachers mentoring African American Boys

Dr. Michael A. Coe, M.Ed, D.Div.

ISBN 978-1-0980-7596-5 (paperback)
ISBN 978-1-0980-7597-2 (digital)

Copyright © 2022 by Dr. Michael A. Coe, M.Ed, D.Div.

All rights reserved. No part of this publication may be reproduced, distributed, or transmitted in any form or by any means, including photocopying, recording, or other electronic or mechanical methods without the prior written permission of the publisher. For permission requests, solicit the publisher via the address below.

Christian Faith Publishing
832 Park Avenue
Meadville, PA 16335
www.christianfaithpublishing.com

Printed in the United States of America

In loving memory of my mother, Betty Herring-Melvin; my maternal grandmother (Mama), Marietta Smith-Bailey; and a special student, Stephon Bacon—may each of you continue to rest in eternal peace.

CONTENTS

Educational Philosophy of Michael Coe 9
Mission Statement 11
Chapter 1: Introduction 13
    Description of the Problem 13
        Demographics 14
    History and Background of the Problem 14
        My personal motivation 15
        Rationale 15
The Plan 17
The Research Question 17
Overview 17
Chapter 2: Literature Review 18
    Introduction 18
    Current research 18
    Various ideas and approaches 19
Black Male Teachers Matter 23
    Do You Know Enough about Me to Teach Me? 24
    Making Policy around This Research Is Complicated 26
        He looks like me 28
        Why America needs more black male teachers 29
        A built-in trust factor 32
        Preparing the mind 32
        African American male leadership 35
    How You Look Is Important 42
    Why Keep Your Son Out of Special Education if He Is Not Disabled? 46
    African American Male Role Models 48

The School-to-Prison Pipeline 49
    What is the school-to-prison pipeline? 50
    Who's in the pipeline? 50
    Punishing policies 51
    Best practices 52
    Avoiding the pipeline 53
    A universal message 54
The Tuskegee of the North 54
Fact 1 56
    Can I really tell you the naked truth? 56
Bring Our Children Home 56
    The Tuskegee of the North 57
School-to-Prison Pipeline Continues 59
Related Resources 60
What is zero tolerance? 64
Origins of zero tolerance 64
Disparities in the application of zero tolerance 65
What Is Restorative Justice? 69
    Fixing the Leaky Classroom Pipeline 73
    Taking action 73
    The voice of African American males 74
        Diversifying our nation's classrooms. 74
Why We Need More Black Men in the Classroom 76
    There must be a call to action 79
Call Me Mister 82
    They need to see someone who likes them. 85
    Get the Facts 86
        Racial disproportionality in school disci-
        pline: Implicit bias Is heavily implicated 86
Chapter 3: Methodology 92
    The Overview 92
    Participants/Demographics 92
    Procedures 93
    Data Collection 93
    Interviews 93
    Student journals 94

	Rap sessions 94	
	Tickets out 94	
	Validity..94	
	Process validity 95	
	Catalytic validity 95	
	Dialogic validity 95	
	Outcome validity 96	
	Limitations..96	
	Summary...96	
Chapter 4:	The Results 98	
	Overview...98	
	Specific Findings 99	
	Student Journals..99	
	Session 1 99	
	Session 2 100	
	Session 3 100	
	Session 4 101	
	Session 5 102	
	Session 6 102	
	Session 7 103	
	Teacher Observation....................................103	
	Summary of Findings 103	
Chapter 5:	Summary..104	
	Overview...104	
	My expectations of the study results.....................104	
	Results in comparison to experts 105	
	The Takeaway from the Research Study................105	
	Validity issues 106	
	Catalytic validity 107	
	What This Research Means for My Teaching..........107	
	Summary...107	

EDUCATIONAL PHILOSOPHY OF MICHAEL COE

My personal philosophy of education arises from a host of feelings, thoughts, and reactions to children. My philosophy of education has evolved over thirteen years: through age, through experience, and particularly through being an active member of our educational community and society. This evolution brings me to believe that all children need the opportunity to develop their own answers and responses to life's questions.

I once believed that students should memorize academic concepts that were held in high regard. Students were diligent in their ability to *regurgitate* facts. Through my own educational evolution, I came to believe that concentrated energy must be spent providing an environment where children can feel comfortable, motivated, and inspired to experiment and explore the varied aspect of the curriculum.

When students are motivated and supported to discover solutions to problems and concepts, they are empowered with tools to obtain knowledge. True learning has taken place! The effect and impression of this experience upon the student will last a lifetime. We have effectively transformed students from repeating ideas to comprehending and understanding the concepts and ideas. Consequently, the student has become *the master* of their individual universe of learning.

The child is reinforced with a positive experience and, thus, will ultimately become an individual who "loves to learn." To achieve this lofty standard, all elements of the educational hierarchy must be carefully put in place, including the superintendent, principal, director, supervisor, teacher, and the student.

This philosophy is aimed at all students, set forth in a system of inclusion, out-of-class replacement (resource), or perhaps the self-contained classroom, whereby all students learn, work, socialize, and reinforce many concepts and ideas through living the experience together. My personal beliefs, as a teacher of special needs students, have provided me with the unique opportunity of observing and participating in the formula of modifying information and restructuring curriculum that allows individuals the choice to learn and the opportunity to grow at their own pace.

The final aspect of my philosophy is the involvement and participation of the family. Incorporating this vital link, the parents help bridge the world and message of our schools to the home. Through the reinforcement of these elements, social and academic milestones are greeted enthusiastically, encouraging growth and a commitment to educational goals we strive to reach with every child we encounter.

MISSION STATEMENT

Education for all students, through discovery and exploration, in an inclusive system, whereby we enrich lives, develop talents and nurture sensitivity, for humankind, through respect and understanding, in a multicultural society.

CHAPTER 1

INTRODUCTION

Description of the Problem

Through the active involvement of volunteering, we can begin to liberate our race from the social, political. Economic and educational ills that affect us.

—Dennis, 1991

I witnessed firsthand the internal destruction of African American males in our society. Nowhere else was this destruction as evident in America as in our urban areas, where drugs, crime, teenaged violence, racial conflict, and poverty were manifesting themselves at such a rapid pace.

Despite the increased education, funds, and programs developed for behavioral modification, not to mention an increase in construction activities for prison systems, these problems were worsening. This was because the real problem lies in the absence of positive role models, including foremost fathers, as well as a spiritual framework, within which African American males can draw reference. This framework should be accompanied by a system of accountability regarding standards, values, and respect for humankind.

Demographics

The setting of this problem was the inner city of Trenton, New Jersey, in the southern section known as the South Ward. I was a special education teacher at Grace A. Dunn Middle School. The school had a population of 763 students, consisting of Latinos (57 percent), African Americans (32 percent), Asians (0.01 percent), Whites (10 percent), Central Americans, and Haitians. Within the student body, 62.8 percent received free lunch, 11.3 percent received reduced meals, and 26 percent of the students paid for lunch. I targeted the African American male population which was eleven to fourteen years old.

In my middle school, this was the low-income group, and many live in private or public rental housing, known to many as the "Southside Projects." Within the family structure of most of these students, there was no presence of a strong male figure. The high school dropout rate was extraordinarily high. In fact, many of the African American males never made it to high school. If they did go, a great number of them dropped out. Senseless violence was on the rise, and drugs became the only means of income and sustenance for the majority.

History and Background of the Problem

The problem was a pressing one as there is generation upon generation of African males who lost their lives because of increased drug use and related criminal actions. There was a loss of fear in the community; many of these young males had no fear of danger or death. They did not even fear God. This left a great sense of hopelessness within the community. The lack of economics and the importance of education were ever so piercing. Many of our youth did not see the need for education, and the problem most often stemmed from their home life. The nuclear family was almost nonexistent in many homes. This plague, which took root in the late 1960s and early 1970s, had shown itself strongly in recent years in the form of drug abuse, drug sales, gangs, and senseless killings. The absence of a responsible father forces our mothers to provide for the family.

This left our African American males with little or no direction and supervision. Regrettably, many were left without a male role model to guide them.

My personal motivation

I witnessed many African American males either cutting class or acting out in the hallway and classroom. Students did not bring assignments, and a vast number of them failed. I was personally concerned for three reasons:

1. Young African American males were dying at a rapid rate because they had no direction. Rather than doing productive activities, they were using and selling drugs or involved in gang wars.
2. Some youth had no respect for other peers or property, which resulted in crimes such as robbery and murder.
3. The death rate in our city had increased, and the dropout rate had more than doubled.
4. My African American brothers were entering the prison system and, for the first time, acquiring a criminal record.

Rationale

The crime rate in the community had tripled within the past few years. African American males had now joined gangs in my city. The Crips and Bloods were now recruiting many of the city's African American males. This association made these young men a target for an early grave. In this respect, many sold their souls to gangs, for it was said that "once in, always in, and the only exit was through death by the way of the grave." I believed if there were more mentoring programs for our inner-city African American males, it would help change the antisocial behavior of our brothers not just in Trenton, New Jersey, but throughout the world as well.

I selected this topic because, as a young African American male growing up in a single female-parent household, I knew what it was like to not have had a positive male role model living under the same roof. I knew the hardships and challenges that African American males face growing up in a single-parent household led by a female parent.

I look back on those years and wept sometimes because of some of the mistakes I had made. If I would've had a strong male figure to guide me during my early teen years, I would have not made many mistakes. I thank God for Uncle Charles and two African American male school teachers whose words helped mold my life. These men change my life. Uncle Charles, the brother of my biological father, treated me as if I was his own son. He invested time in teaching me about honesty, how to develop a good work ethic, and the responsibilities of a man. The teachers encouraged me to stay in school and study hard. These men helped change my life.

Mr. Sweets and Mr. Powell were African American male teachers who mentored me during my middle- and high school years. They taught me I had to have endurance and a vision in order to become someone in life. Many times, they would talk with me regarding the plight of the African American male. Mr. Powell was my brick mason teacher and would hire me to work with him during the summer. They often reminded me that many of our African American males are in jail or in the grave because they had no vision.

Many of our children are living in single-parent household because many of our men have refused to take responsibility for their actions. They taught me that any male could make a baby, but it would take a man to accept the responsibility of raising that child. I thank God they often reminded me that education was the key to my future and that the only person who could stop me from successfully using and achieving my God-given ability would be *me*.

Today, I am grateful to the Almighty God that these men devoted their time to guide me in the right direction. It is because of them that my life has been enriched.

The Plan

The Research Question

The question that will guide my research is, How does teacher mentoring decrease the antisocial behaviors of black African American males in an inner-city middle school? What compelled me to ask this question was my own personal concern and interest in the African American male. I witnessed increased African American male gang involvement and constant suspensions from school, as well as a lack of self-respect in these young men. It saddened me to see my people traveling hopelessly in life to a dead end. It was my hope that during this sixteen-week study, I might provide proper direction for those young men through the use of this research project.

Overview

Chapter 1 provides the title and background of the research. It included my personal feelings, background, and interest in the selection of mentoring the African American male in the inner-city school.

Chapter 2 provided a review of the literature on information about what experts say in regard to my topic: The decrease of antisocial behavior of African American males in the inner-city middle school as affected by teacher mentoring.

Chapter 3 focuses on the methods of data collection used in the teacher research project.

Chapter 4 provides the results of my finding in the data collected over the eight-week period.

Chapter 5 offers an overview of my findings and discusses the results of my research. It includes the changes that have taken place in the life of the students and how they were impacted by the study. A summary of whether the study was a success, reasons for the continuing of the study in the future, and personal reflections are be provided.

CHAPTER 2

LITERATURE REVIEW

Introduction

This chapter contains the literary review of gathered factual data concerning the most recent trend, statistics, and data on the subject of mentoring the African American male.

Current research

In an effort to determine suitable programs for African American males at risk, it's been discovered that there are several research and pilot programs that targeted the subject of African American males from advanced research studies to grassroot efforts by an organization for African American males.

Christianity Today published an article entitled "Teaching Manhood in the Urban Jungle" (1997). This article was written regarding a program entitled the Simba Program, which focused on teaching African American males what it means to be a believer in God and oneself. The name *Simba* is Swahili and means to be a believer in God and oneself. It also means lion, which represents the character of men. The program concentrated on transcending the negative stereotypes placed on African American males by media.

The program taught the African American male about manhood in terms of violent acts committed, sexual promiscuity, and a life of substance abuse. Researchers stated Simba sends a different message to African American males in the efforts they need to understand. The program forced African American males to take the entire negative he has ever identified with and though redefinition of himself. Through various steps in the program, he realizes his experiences, and he sees a new person emerging, with confidence, possibility, and positive rather than negative tendencies.

A strong and powerful statement was made by an African American student: "I know I'm going to achieve something with my life because the teachers/mentors in Simba keep reminding me that I can and I will."

Various ideas and approaches

Approaches within the past several years have been diverse and specifically tailored to target the urban African American male population. Houses of worship, human service organizations, and corporate America all are concerned and ready to assist in a vital role in the preservation of this endangered culture species. The majority of these programs seek to empower the African American male through these vital principles of visitation, interaction, and training.

Black Enterprise magazine (1997) published an article entitled "Saving Black Youth." Faced with a soaring body count of African American males struck down by violence, statistics cited that African American males which made up 12 percent of the twenty thousand people who died were victims in homicides annually. The age groups of these homicide victims are thirteen and twenty-four years of age. Statistics indicated that the African American male population is one of the most distressed in our society (2005).

Harvard Professor Noguera (2003) suggested that African American males are in deep trouble. Noguera stated that African American males lead the nation in homicides, both as victims and perpetrators and in what observers regarded as an alarming trend; they now have the fastest growing rate for suicide. For the last several years, African American males have contracted HIV and AIDS at a faster rate than any other segment of the population, and their incarceration, conviction, and arrest rates have been at the top of the charts in most states for some time.

Noguera also stated that African American males in education with respect to attainment and academic performance also showed signs of trouble and distress. It is stated that in many school districts throughout the United States, African American males are more likely to be suspended and expelled from school than any other group.

However, Kao, and Tienda (1998) and Hauser and Anderson (1991) shared considerable evidence that the vast majority of African American males would like to do well in school. Additionally, there are schools where academic success for African American males is the norm and not the exception (Sizemore 1998, Edmonds 1979). Both facts provide a basis for hope that achievement patterns can be reversed if there is a willingness to provide the resources and support to create the conditions that nurture academic success.

Noguera (2001) stated in his findings that some schools in Northern California have consistent evidence from black students who value education and would like to succeed in school (February 11, 2002). Ninety percent of the African American males stated that they agreed with the statement, "That they thought that education is important, and they wanted to go to college." However, studies have shown that when students were asked about the teacher and the support that they received, some indicated that they did not think their teachers offer meaningful or noticeable support.

Researchers revealed if students do not believe that the adults who teach them care about them and are actively concerned about their academic performance, the likelihood that they will succeed is greatly reduced (Noguera 2003). *In the Metropolitan Life Annual Survey* on teaching, 39 percent of 3,961 students stated that they trusted their teachers. It was even more telling that when the data from the survey was disaggregated by race and class. Minority and poor students indicated significantly higher levels of distrust (47 percent of minorities and 53 percent of poor students stated that they trusted their teachers only a little or not at all (MetLife Survey 2000).

Though it is still possible that some students will succeed even if they do not trust or feel supported by their teachers, research on teacher expectation suggests that they generally have powerful effects on students' performance (Weinstein 2000).

Researchers Ladson-Billing, Foster, and Lee have suggested that more than other students, the performance of African American males is influenced to a large degree by the social support and encouragement they receive from teachers (Ladson-Billing 1994, Foster 1997, Lee 2004). To the extent that this is true, and if the nature of interactions between many African American males and their teachers tends to be negative, it is unlikely that it will be possible to elevate their achievement without changing the way in which they are treated by teachers (Edmonds 2000).

Professor Melissa Roderick stated that African American males often do not feel cared for in their school communities. She stated that this was the most devastating factor for African American males (Mickelson 1989).

However, researcher Edmonds (Sizemore 1988, Murphy and Hallinger 1998) has indicated that there were schools where African American male students do well, and high levels of achievement are common. In his studies, it was revealed that in California Public Schools, there are twenty-two schools in the state where African American male students comprised 50 percent or more of the student population which have aggregate scores of 750 or greater on state examinations (University of California Report of Black Student Achievement). These students in these public schools are high achievers. Researchers for years have studied effective schools and have found that such schools possess the following characteristics:

1. A clear sense of purpose
2. Core standards within a rigorous curriculum
3. High expectations
4. Commitment to educate all students
5. Safe and orderly learning environment
6. Strong partnership with parents
7. A problem-solving attitude

Leading researcher Ron Edmonds stated that "we already know more than enough to successfully educate all students…the question is whether we want to teach all students" (Edmonds 1979).

Research indicated that most African American males were not enrolled in effective schools that nurture and support them while simultaneously providing high-quality instruction. Since these were the overwhelming majority of African American males, other strategies have been devised to produce support even as pressure was exerted upon schools to change.

It was stated that children who have the good fortune to attend good schools will eventually become adults who find themselves working in environments that are less supportive and perhaps even hostile. Researchers stated that these students will also need to learn how to cope with adversity and to navigate the overt and covert forms of discrimination they will encounter.

McPartland and Nettles (1999) have stated that parents have turned to churches and community organizations as a possible source of such support (McPartland and Nettles 1999). Organizations such as Simba (a mentoring program for black African American males) and the Omega Boys Club have stepped in and provided African American males with academic support and adult mentoring in and outside the school (Watson and Smitherman 1996).

Researchers Ampim and Meyers have stated organizations like these have helped affirm the identities of African American males by providing them with knowledge and information about African and African American History and culture and instilled a sense of social responsibility towards their families and communities.

In the last decade, I have witnessed the destruction of African American males. And in order to make a positive impact in the life of African American males in inner-city schools, the students must feel that they can trust their teacher. African Americans must feel safe and comfortable in order to share what is in their lives. The teacher must understand that trust is not given but is gained from the student, and in order to have a successful relationship, this must take place.

Black Male Teachers Matter

James E. Causey shared these findings in the *Milwaukee Journal Sentinel*:

> A recent study found that black students who have at least one black teacher do better in school. One of the most stubborn problems in K-12 education is the academic achievement gap between white students and students of color, particularly Black students. And both data and anecdotal evidence suggest that teachers of color are in singular positions to move the dial on black student performance.
>
> Having at least one Black teacher in elementary school cuts the high school dropout rates of very low-income Black boys 39% and raises college aspirations among poor students of both sexes by 19%, according to a 2017 study by researchers from Johns Hopkins University, American University and the University of California, Davis.
>
> In other words, students of color, particularly African American males, respond to people who look like them leading classrooms. The problem, in Milwaukee and elsewhere, is that black male teachers are a rarity. Nationwide, Black teachers make up less than 7% of all teachers; Black men make up 2%
>
> Research showed in Wisconsin, Milwaukee Public Schools is the state's largest district, with roughly 75,000 students. More than 40,000, or 54%, are African American, according to 2018-19 school data. A little more than 20,000, or 27%, are Hispanic. Barely 8,000, or 11%, are white. However, 71% of MPS (Special

Education) teachers are white, almost three out of every four. Black male teachers make up just 2% Statewide, 9% of all students are African American, but only 2% of state teachers and 5% of principals are African American, according to a 2019 *University of Wisconsin-Milwaukee study*. The problem is particularly acute in special education, according to a commentary published in the journal Perspectives on Urban Education by LaRon A. Scott, an associate professor of counseling and special education at *Virginia Commonwealth University*, and Marcus Turner, Angela Peterson/Milwaukee Journal Sentinel.

Statewide, 9% of all students are African American, but only 2% of state teachers and 5% of principals are African American, according to a 2019 *University of Wisconsin-Milwaukee study*.

The problem is particularly acute in special education, according to a commentary published in the journal Perspectives on Urban Education by LaRon A. Scott, an associate professor of counseling and special education at *Virginia Commonwealth University*.

Do You Know Enough about Me to Teach Me?

In urban public schools, most children in special education are black, and they are overwhelmingly taught by white women. Those teachers report that they "felt poorly prepared to work with black children," Scott said. Additionally, black boys who go through schools without engaging with a black male teacher are "denied perspectives, guidance, and an understanding that may only come from a black male teacher," Scott said. While there are many areas of improvement that we could look at changing for more successful outcomes for black men, I will discuss just four indicators that illustrate the current situation for black boys in the United States, with the hope of starting a conversation about what we can do to produce a stronger generation of black young men in our society.

1. *Black boys are more likely to be placed in special education.*

While it is true that black boys often arrive in kindergarten classrooms with inherent disadvantages, they continue to experience a "behind the eight ball" mentality as their school careers progress. Black boys are more likely than any other group to be placed in special education classes, with 80 percent of all special education students being African American males or Hispanic males.

Learning disabilities are just a part of the whole picture. Black students (and particularly boys) experience disconnection when it comes to the authority figures in their classrooms. The K–12 teaching profession is dominated by white women, many of whom are very qualified and very interested in helping all their students succeed but lack the firsthand experience needed to connect with their black male students

2. *Black boys are more likely to attend schools without the adequate resources to educate them.*

Schools with a majority of black students tend to have lower numbers of teachers who are certified in their degree areas. A United States Department of Education report found that in schools with at least 50 percent black students, only 48 percent were certified in the subject, compared with 65 percent in schools with a white majority. In English, the numbers were 59 and 68 percent, respectively; and in science, they were 57 percent and 73 percent.

3. *Black boys are not reading at an adequate level.*

In 2014, the Black Star Project published findings that just 10 percent of eighth-grade black boys in the United States are considered "proficient" in reading. In urban areas like Chicago and Detroit, that number was even lower. By contrast, the 2013 National Assessment of Education Progress found that 46 percent of white students are adequate readers by eighth grade, and 17 percent of black students as a whole are too. The achievement gap between the two races is startling, but the difference between the NAEP report on black students as a whole and the Black Star Project findings of just black boys is troubling too. It is not simply black children in general who appear to be failing in the basics—like literacy; it is the boys.

Reading is only one piece of the school puzzle, of course, but it is a foundational one. If the eighth graders in our schools cannot read, how will they ever learn other subjects and make it to a college education (or, in reality, to a high school diploma)? Reading scores tell us so much more than the confines of their statistics. I believe these numbers are key to understanding the plight of young black men in our society as a whole.

4. *Punishment for black boys is harsher than for any other demographics.*

Punishment for black boys—even first-time offenders—in schools is harsher than for any other demographics. Consider these facts:

Black students make up just 18 percent of children in United States preschools but make up half of those youngsters who are suspended.

Black boys receive two-thirds of all school suspensions nationwide—all demographics and both genders considered.

Making Policy around This Research Is Complicated

McCall says her identity has been crucial for her students at César E. Chávez Multicultural Academic Center on the south side of Chicago.

Having a black teacher allows students to see people who look like them in positions of influence," she says. "Students believe they can assume their own roles of authority."

McCall's perception is backed by new academic research. A recent study published by the Institute of Labor Economics found that if a low-income black male student in third, fourth, or fifth grade has a black teacher, he is 39 percent less likely to drop out of high school. And if a low-income black male or female student of the same age has a black teacher (especially of the same gender), they are more likely to plan to attend a four-year college. Females were 19 percent more likely to express this intent while males were 29 percent more likely. The benefit came from having just one black teacher; having two or more black teachers did not alter the results.

Yet teachers of color are a relative rarity. The National Education Association has found that while students of color make up almost half of the public school population, teachers of color comprise only 16 percent of all teachers. Black teachers are also more likely to be clustered in high-need economically disadvantaged urban schools. While all of this holds true, it is imperative that more black males are hired, especially in the district I work and nationally.

The question becomes then, How do we hire more black male teachers and get them in the right classrooms? I firmly believe that having a black male teacher in education is needed. I personally have had many of my former male students visit me over time and have thanked me for being hard on them. Although they didn't appreciate it at the time, however, now that they are adults, they realized had it not been for me, they most likely would have dropped out of school.

When the new research on black teachers was first released, it provoked some controversy over this question. Seth Gershenson, a coauthor of the study and professor of public policy at American University, says that he and his coauthors fielded a number of incredulous messages on social media asking whether they were advocating for desegregation.

Research has proven if a low-income black male student in third, fourth, or fifth grade has a black teacher, he is 39 percent less likely to drop out of high school. I am living proof that having a black male teacher helps the black male to achieve or excel academically. Seeing some who look like me make difference.

Some have interpreted the study's results as *proof that integration is not an effective tool* to address the achievement gap between black and white students. Rafiq Kalam Id-Din, a cofounder of the Ember Charter School for Mindful Education in Brooklyn, says that the research confirms that putting black and brown students with wealthy white peers and teachers doesn't bring about better academic outcomes for them.

"Integration doesn't address the roots of the problem," he says, noting that white teachers and administrators fail to appropriately consider and account for the culture and life experiences of children of color. "Black teachers are far more apt to do this instructionally." As such, Ember's staff, which teaches a student body that is a majority of color, is 95 percent black and Latino.

But Gershenson and his colleagues emphasize that segregating students is not to take away from their study, nor is it the message they want to send. Indeed, the academic community broadly argues that racial balance in education is good for students of color as well as white students. "For instance," Gershenson says, "while it isn't covered in our study, social science research shows that white kids also benefit from having a black teacher because it counters their biases."

Gershenson says researchers have not entirely unpacked all the reasons why same-race teachers matter for black students. But dynamics such as the role model effect play a central role.

He looks like me

Most education experts agree that all students benefit from regular exposure to black teachers, and when present in schools, they are also often perceived as more approachable and voted most popular among students from all backgrounds. Still, the exceptionally low number of African American men in America's classrooms is not about winning popularity contests; many education experts assert it's a matter of educational equity or the lack thereof. It is well-documented that black students, who are regularly cited for lagging behind their white counterparts academically, actually perform better when taught by teachers of the same race. African American boys need to see a teacher who looks like them. Why? It's a matter of life and death.

"Kids do better when they're taught by teachers who look like them specially African American males That's just the way it is," education professor David Kretschmer said, California State University, Northridge (CSUN), one of two directors leading the Future Minority Male Teachers Across California Project, known as F2MTC, which aims to recruit, prepare, and retain male teachers of color at the elementary level throughout California's university system. "That's why we need more African American males of color in America's classrooms, period."

Why America needs more black male teachers

My students know I am going to push them. It does not matter if they are black, white, or whatever; I try to tell them about the things I've learned in life. In my tenure, I came to understand they're not looking for someone perfect; they just want someone who keeps it real.

It's not strictly anecdotal. A growing body of recent research asserts that the presence of a black man in the classroom is both rare and critically needed in American public schools.

Since 2014, ethnic and racial minorities make up more than half of the student population in United States public schools, yet about 80 percent of teachers are white and 77 percent of them are female. People of color make up about 20 percent of teachers; a mere 2 percent are black men.

To this point, a groundbreaking 2017 study coauthored by a Johns Hopkins University economist found that having just one African American teacher in elementary school significantly increased a low-income black student's likelihood of graduating from high school and considering college; for a very low-income black boy, the risk of dropping out was reduced by 39 percent.

Jackson says he's not surprised. When he's not trying to build rapport with his students on the playing field as a coach or in his career readiness and computer skills classes, he said, he attempts to do so by joking with them around campus. The interaction, he believes, helps them feel more positively about school, and they also tend to open up more about problems.

"I hate to say it, but as a black male teacher, you always kind of feel like you're under a microscope, like you have to prove yourself," Jackson explained. "I think having that experience helps make you a more approachable person [to students] in general. You know what it's like to feel that pressure. All you want is the best for your students; you just want to see them succeed."

Charles King says those same feelings of support and camaraderie he received from the many black men in leadership at his virtually all-black middle school in Atlanta in the mid-2000s set a strong foundation for his education. He said he didn't fully realize the impact of having so many strong black male educators at KIPP WAYS Academy until he attended an affluent, predominantly white boarding high school in Rome, Georgia, where there were just a few black male teachers. King said his experience at both schools inspired him to earn a bachelor's degree in middle grades education. Four years ago, he returned to his middle school alma mater as a teacher.

Charles King teaches seventh-grade English and says he connects with his students on a "higher level."

"I realized that I wanted my students to have access to the same resources that I had," recalled King, twenty-five, who teaches seventh-grade English. "I feel like I can connect with my students on a higher level because of our shared identity. I think they know—they can feel it—that I want the best for them. Being in the classroom is also a great opportunity for them to see a different version of a black man, the human side of a black man, and not the negative stereotypes that they usually see when they turn on the TV."

King says he feels very supported at his school (the KIPP charter school network is well-known for its diverse teacher workforce). However, many African American male teachers nationwide, especially where there are smaller numbers, say for them, not so much. Many report feelings isolated, passed over for decision-making positions, and forced into disciplinary roles, particularly for students of color.

Research has also found that African American male teachers are disproportionately clustered in under-resourced schools with fewer opportunities for mentorship and professional development, which often contributes to burnout and high attrition levels. Vincent Cobb, Rashiid Coleman, and Sterling Grimes are leading a Philadelphia-based program charged with changing that. *The Fellowship: Black Male Educators for Social Justice* started in 2014 with the objective of adding one thousand black male educators, or BMEs, to city public schools by 2025. "We're at 648; we started at 348," Coleman said.

The Fellowship also hosts regional and national gatherings for black male teachers from across the country for networking opportunities and access to job fairs, mentorship programs, and professional development.

"We're here to let black men know that teaching is an opportunity to make a real difference, whether you live in a small town or a major metropolitan area," Cobb explained, The Fellowship's CEO. "Our kids are screaming out for help. We're trying to spark a movement."

The Fellowship is one of the dozens of initiatives nationwide focused on recruiting and retaining black male teachers. For example, historically black Southern University of New Orleans' *Honoré Center for Undergraduate Student Achievement* offers full scholarships in exchange for a two-year teaching commitment.

James Ford, who taught history and sociology in a Charlotte, North Carolina, high school for six years, said his mere presence made a difference to the students he taught. "I'm a black man with dreadlocks. The moment I set foot in the classroom, I instantly show the possibilities available to them," he said. Ford adds that his background allowed him to reach his students more effectively. "If there was a concept that was difficult to comprehend," he says, "I would use Ebonics, and it instantly gave the kids access to ideas they had never heard explained in a language they understand."

I agree with James Ford. As a black male teacher, it is much easier for students to learn in my class because I develop a trust relationship with my students. I meet them at a place where they are. What I mean by that is that I can identify with them. I know the culture, I speak their language, I cry like they cry, I feel their hurt, but I am that one living example that they see 180 days a year. Why? I understand the culture of the students in my class. I am an African American male who has gone through similar experiences.

A built-in trust factor

African American male teachers build different kinds of relationships with their students because they have experienced things that white teachers just do not experience. I learned a lot about myself and young people on that first year. I saw how the boys responded to me. It was different. They just seemed to listen more, and I did not need to raise my voice. In saying this, it has a lot to do with our culture—the black culture.

Preparing the mind

At the beginning of the school year for the last twenty years, I prepared my classroom with an inviting atmosphere. My classroom is not your normal classroom. I select books and novels that my students can identify with (relate to). I have reading centers around my room. I have framed black art and quotes throughout the room. I have created relaxing reading centers. One center has a sofa with a rug on the floor so the students can relax and read. I selected the *Bluford Series*, a series of novels that are written for inner-city students. These novels share stories of inner-city students and what they encounter living in the inner city.

When my students arrive, they arrive at a welcoming atmosphere, a clean room, and music playing. Each of them is greeted by their last name with the mister or misses. I knew each student who walks through the doors of my classroom knew if he/she did not have breakfast or did not have a grab-and-go. There is always healthy food in my room for them. I strongly believe if I am going to make an impact, it cannot be done when a student did not have breakfast. No one can go on an empty stomach. As I stated, classroom atmosphere plays a big role in student achievement. My motto is, "Look your best, do you best, and be your best!"

I am preparing my students for the future. As an African American male teacher, I am more than a teacher. I am a role model.

When my students see me, they see a person who lived in their neighbors or one like theirs. They see a living and talking story that made it out of poverty. They see an African American male who is not hanging on the corner and does not wear his pants sagging. When they see me, I want them to see themselves possibly ten years from that day.

I purposely come to school dressed in the latest styles of fashion so they can see how a black male should dress. I don't come to school with designer-label clothing because it is not about showing a designer label. I want them to see it's not about designer labels. I tell my students they can have anything they want in life, but my job as their teacher is to usher them into real education and to unfold as much knowledge to them. "Knowledge is power!"

My role as an African American male educator is far more important than standing in front of a class. I have been given the task to make a positive and everlasting impact on the life of each student who enters my class. My role in my students' lives as a black male in the front of a class goes far beyond that of a teacher.

My students know they have an advocate who looks like them and who has literally sat in their seats. I show my students' tough love and compassion while preparing them for the future. My students understand they have a person who fights for their rights, giving them the best possibilities of achieving their goals.

When I share my childhood story with male students, it allows them to see another side of me that they would never imagine. This dialog causes them to look through different lenses. They become vulnerable and transparent, allowing me to instill knowledge and empower them holistically as I mentioned previously.

Moreover, my students see the possibility to be successful despite their current living conditions and circumstances around them. Many students discover where they want to go in life, and together, we are constantly striving toward each unique goal. Together, we are resilient, breaking down barriers, combating stereotypes, and reaching new levels of success in and out of the classroom. It's a sense of family when students arrive in my class; they know that they are valued, respected, safe, and treated like family.

In the last twenty years (decade), I have witnessed the destruction of African American males; and to make a positive impact in the life of African American males in the inner-city schools, the student must feel that he can trust his teacher. Students must feel safe and comfortable sharing what is going on in their lives. The teacher must understand that trust is not given, but it is gained from the student; and to have a successful relationship, this must take place.

To be effective, one must become a good listener and not always say what comes to mind. The teacher must be able to open and share his thoughts with his students to build that trust.

It has been stated in scientific research that same-race teachers can also affect relations with parents. "Black parents are more comfortable dealing with a black teacher than a white teacher, and the benefit of this shows up in their greater involvement in school." Such parents' children, he adds, have higher attendance rates and lower suspension rates.

As a child growing up in a rural country town in the sixties, it was separate schools for blacks and whites in my small town of Elizabethtown, North Carolina. I was fortunate to have several African American male teachers, and I can say, those teachers made a lasting impact on my life. I shall never forget those great African American male educators. In the late sixties, things changed because integration took place, and I saw few African American male teachers.

I was inspired to do my master's thesis research and pen this book because of the impact African American male teachers made in my life. I had the privilege to sit in a classroom with someone who looked like me and who had more experience in the world than I did.

Their instructions to me were to get an education because society would not be fair to me. As an African American male student, they made sure I knew the subject matter and pass their class. If I received an A, I earned that A. I can recall one marking period when my average was a point away from having an A. I was upset because

I just knew because I was Mr. Powell's best student, and his student assistant surely I thought he would have given me just one point to make an A. Needless to say, he didn't! He said, "Life is not going to give you anything. You must earn it." In the next marking period, I studied harder; and in the next marking period, I earned an A. I adopted the same philosophy in my classroom. My students know that if they want an A, they must do the work to earn that grade.

Those great teachers knew what life was going to bring my way. Mr. Powell said, "Be the best that you can, and always know that you were born with two strikes against you." My question was, What are those strikes?

He said, "You are a black, and you are a male in society, and this world will try to hold you back, but having an education will be the tools you need to compete in a biased society." I want to echo this again. Having positive black male teachers in my life impacted my life in such a way that I can't really express. Thanks to all my fellow African American male teachers who are paving the way for our young black boys.

I started teaching eighth-grade special needs students who were in a general education class, which we call inclusion. My students would take science and social studies with general education students for those two subjects. I taught them math and language arts. They were in my resource class. During my twenty years, I have taught all four major subjects in a self-contain classroom with boys and girls. I wanted to make an even greater impact. I requested an all-male class; needless to say, this was the beginning of an adventure in life. I gave birth to an ideal that changed the lives of every young male who walks through the doors of my classroom: African American, Caucasian, Hispanic, Mexican, and Indian. This journey as an educator and mentor has been challenging and rewarding.

African American male leadership

In the twenty years that I have been in education, it is rare that even in the district where I work, there are not enough African

American male teachers, and there are even few African American male administrators.

My district seems to cater to women and places them in the key leadership role over African American males. This type of leadership sets a bad example for African American males. African American males need to see African American men in key roles of leadership in the schools. Our African American males in the inner city are raised in single-female-parent homes. They see the domination of female leadership at home and school. The lack of an African American male, I strongly believe, sends a very confusing message as to their role in society.

I believe that if we are going to save the young African American male, changes must be made in the hiring and recruitment of African American male teachers in the inner city. Particularly urgent, Gershenson says, "it is retaining teachers because black teachers exit the profession in greater numbers than white teachers. Because they often face more challenges in high-need schools, they experience burnout more frequently." What Gershenson said is 100 percent true, and, should I add, the pay scale for new teachers must be higher if we are going to attract black males.

This change can be made first with our elective officials and school board member. It is a known fact any city that what to attract new residents must have great schools and great teachers. It's the only way to attract any teacher. Changes must be made because our children need to see positive black males in our society. What better place than in the classroom? They need to see a teacher with the same color skin. They need to experience a black male who speaks correctly and use street lingo if needed. They need to see African American males who look like them and can relate to them.

On January 9, 2017, Gershenson says that though recruitment and hiring is an important goal, the "pipeline problem" makes it difficult. "There are fewer black students entering college who could be black teachers," he says. "Getting more black students on that path is a long-term goal, but if that's all we worry about, it will be too little, too late. Social science research shows that white kids also benefit from having an African American teacher because it counters their biases."

Teacher mentoring is an excellent approach to changing the plight of our young African American males. It can change their direction in life, and it can save their life by keeping them from becoming the property of the state.

As evidenced by former President Barack Obama's My Brother's Keeper (MBK) initiative, our society has recognized the need to provide more mentoring to boys of color. Specifically, mentoring is one of four key interventions of the MBK alliance in order to address the needs and opportunity gaps (e.g., in education) of boys of color.

In August 2016, researchers shared their results on the subject of mentoring for black boys and organized these into the following four topics: (a) its documented effectiveness; (b) the extent to which mentor, youth, and program characteristics influence effectiveness; (c) the processes that link mentoring to outcomes in black male youth; and (d) the extent to which efforts to provide mentoring for African American male youth have reached and engaged these youth, been implemented with high quality, and been adopted and sustained by a host of organizations and settings.

Both formal and informal teacher mentoring/mentoring have the potential to benefit black boys in a range of areas, including academics (e.g., grades), social-emotional well-being (e.g., relationships with others), mental health (e.g., alcohol use), and preventing risky behaviors (e.g., sexual activity).

- Cultural mistrust may influence black boys' perceptions of their white mentors and thus the quality of their relationships with them.
- Mentoring may be able to lessen the negative effects of racial discrimination on black boys.
- Group mentoring approaches seem to support black male youth's social-emotional development through group processes (e.g., unity, brotherhood, trust).
- Mentoring that promotes black boys' racial identity may in turn lead to positive effects in other aspects of their lives

(e.g., academic outcomes). This process may be facilitated by connecting black male youth with mentors who have shared life experiences; engaging black men as mentors has the potential to be useful in this regard although it should be noted that research to inform the possible merits of this strategy is largely lacking.
- Research suggests that black men are more likely to serve as informal rather than formal mentors and that they experience barriers to serving as mentors in formal mentoring programs.
- Developing close and supportive mentoring relationships may be a mechanism by which mentoring promotes positive outcomes in black boys.
- Implications for practice that draw on implications for practice that draws on the findings and conclusions of the review are provided. These include recommendations to do the following:
    o Recognize that black boys are likely to vary in their individual needs and, thus, in the specific types of mentoring supports that might be most effective.
    o Take care to ensure that mentors of black boys receive appropriate training about issues of race, culture, and gender.
    o Recruit mentors with appropriate skills (e.g., teaching or advocacy experience) and cultural competency to mentor black boys effectively.
    o Consider activities and strategies that help black boys to identify, and increase support from, the existing mentoring and resources they have in their lives.
    o Consider how efforts to provide mentoring for black boys can be linked to the fight for larger social justice goals for these youth and their communities.

A report from the White House Council of Economic Advisers explores the barriers that disadvantaged youth face, particularly young men of color, and quantifies the enormous costs this poses to the United States economy. This report focuses on the significant disparities in education, exposure to the criminal justice system, and employment issues that persist among young African males and other males of color and other races of men.

The report outlines why it's important for our nation—from businesses, faith organizations, and civic leaders, and local law enforcement—to invest in the lives of our nation's African American males and males of color. In launching the My Brother's Keeper initiative, former President Obama and his entire administration did just that.

- Getting a healthy start and entering school ready to learn: All children should have a healthy start and enter school ready—cognitively, physically, socially, and emotionally.
- Reading at grade level by third grade: All children should be reading at grade level by age 8—the age at which reading to learn becomes essential.
- Graduating from high school ready for college and career: All youth should receive a quality high school education and graduate with the skills and tools needed to advance to postsecondary education or training.
- Completing postsecondary education or training: Every American should have the option to attend postsecondary education and receive the education and training needed for the quality jobs of today and tomorrow.
- Successfully entering the workforce: Anyone who wants a job should be able to get a job that allows them to support themselves and their families.
- Keeping kids on track and giving them second chances: All youth and young adults should be safe from violent crime, and individuals who are confined should receive the education, training, and treatment they need for a second chance.

The following list below has a wealth of information to support the importance of mentoring:

- April 1, 2016: New Announcements Helping to Achieve MBK Goals by Doing What Works
- February 29, 2016: Two Years of My Brother's Keeper: Building Lasting Bridges of Opportunity for Young People
- February 28, 2016: Engaging America's Youth in STEM through Hands-on Experiences in Labs and Communities Across America
- February 24, 2016: Absences Add Up: New Chronic Absenteeism Campaign Works to Get Kids to Class, and to Graduation
- February 23, 2016: US Department of Education Takes Action to Deliver Equity for Students with Disabilities
- February 19, 2016: The White House Launches New National Effort and Ad Council Campaign to Eliminate Chronic Absenteeism and Drive Student Success
- January 18, 2016: Honoring Dr. Martin Luther King Jr. By Planting the Seeds of Service and Citizenship
- November 2, 2015: Fact Sheet: President Obama Announces New Actions to Promote Rehabilitation and Reintegration for the Formerly Incarcerated
- July 14, 2015: Restoring Hope and Closing Opportunity Gaps
- June 19, 2015: President Obama to Young Men of Color: "You Matter. You Count."

As an educator, I firmly believe it is vital that we embrace and understand the importance of teacher mentoring for African American males, our boys of color. When all stakeholders embrace mentoring, we can shut down the school-to-prison pipeline. I want every reader to understand the advantages and benefits of mentoring. Mentoring has shown to be one of the most valuable and effective development opportunities for students.

Having the guidance, encouragement, and support of a trusted and experienced mentor can provide a mentee (student) with a broad range of personal and life-changing benefits, which ultimately lead to improved performance in the student's life. The advantages of teacher mentoring/mentoring extend to all involved in the program.

Listed below are the sixteen advantages and benefits to all stakeholders.

Advantages for student mentees

1. Develops a skill or competency for student
2. Improves the mentee's confidence in their ability to execute the task at hand
3. Helps the mentee improve their communication skills
4. Gives the mentee practice in accepting feedback from a consistent source
5. Teaches the mentee how to maintain a professional relationship
6. Expands the mentee's network of contacts
7. Provides a crash course on the current life culture

Advantages for teacher mentors

8. Strengthens the mentor's active listening skills
9. Provides a conduit for the mentor to give back to the organization
10. Knowledge shared by the mentor is encouraged, which increases the mentor's sense of self-worth
11. Establishes a sense of fulfillment through teaching
12. Helps enhance the mentor's own relationship-building skills
13. Provides an added sense of purpose and responsibility for one's life.

Advantages for the school district or organization

14. Helps achieve their talent development goals such as succession planning and ensuring solid leadership development

15. Informs everyone throughout the school that teachers are willing to invest in students
16. Harnesses the power of natural leadership

Today, formal African American male mentoring programs can enhance the effectiveness of talent management strategies.

A tailored African American male teacher mentoring/mentoring program will transform us in a plethora of efficient ways.

> Mentoring is critical if we intend to address much of the pain, abuse and abandonment that African American males suffer from. While we struggle to find mentors for young African American males, it is equally important to locate the fathers of these young brothers. A young boy's first mentor should be his father and the other men in his family. Responsible fatherhood must be viewed as a necessary action step to begin the healing process among African American males.

If we cannot locate his father, then we as African American males and African American male teachers must become his surrogate father. The Africa Proverb declares, "It takes a village to raise a child."

How You Look Is Important

I have always loved fashion for as long as I can remember. One thing my grandmother taught me is to always be clean and look your best. I share with students in my class the importance of doing your best, being your best, and looking your best. Daily, I share with my students, especially the males, that your image is a representation of what you have to offer to society.

Over the last twenty years in education, I have worked closely with the male population, living in a day of sagging pants and crazy hairstyles that our youth adopt from NBA players who are millionaires who will most likely never have to go on an interview for a job. The image that much of what they portray is not good for our youth in general. Young boys idolize these NBA and NFL players and other famous images seen on television.

When working with African American males, I show them what we portray and what we should portray.

The one thing many African American males are not taught growing up is the importance of their image. Some African American males either don't care or don't know what their image does for their lives. As a result, they become inattentive and do not care what they wear.

Therefore, I constructed a sample wardrobe for the black male to benefit them in all situations and events.

It's known that a person is judged within ten seconds of meeting someone. It's not always what you know in life but what others think of you that creates opportunities. What I tried to instill in my students is the importance of good hygiene and how they look.

Boyz 2 Men is a mentoring group I started twenty years ago for African American males and boys of color. In this program, I shared with the young men some of my life experiences. I developed trust with them. When they felt they could trust me, they opened up to me. They shared some personal things. I assured them that what we discussed would stay between us unless there was something that would cause them harm.

During our first session, I shared with young men the importance of personal hygiene and taking care of themselves. This discussion was important because as teenagers they were experiencing puberty. As we all know, young boys at this age don't really like to take baths or shower. During this session, we had some laughs, but it was a rewarding time for me as well as for them. We covered a wide range of topics during our sessions. In another session, I shared about table etiquette with the students, its rules and manners, the *do*s and *don't*s while dining at a dinner table, and how to properly set a table; they were later quizzed.

I presented a challenge to all students: Those who scored more than 90 percent would be treated to dinner, but they must be dressed for the occasion. Well, to my surprise, they all scored 90 percent and above. I guess one might say being taken out to dinner was worth it!

The next assigned task was teaching them the importance of looking presentable at all times other than playing. I knew this task would be an even great challenge. It was going to cause them to come out of their comfort zone. Knowing the life of many of the inner-city children, many of them didn't own dress clothing. I sent a letter home, soliciting parents' help. Each student had worn a shirt and tie. They were picked up by my driver in a limousine driven by a chauffeur. What a night it was just to see the faces of these young African Americans from inner-city underprivileged males being picked by a limousine and taken out to dinner. It wasn't something any of them ever experienced.

I established Power Mondays. Every Monday, all students were required to report to school in business professional attire. For boys, this meant a shirt, tie, slacks, shoes, and a belt. Now that the students looked professional, I wanted them to feel professional as well. Each Monday morning, right after the morning announcements, I would take an entire grade level of our male students to the cafeteria, where we participated in a presentation and discussion led by one or more male staff members and men from the community whom we had recruited to be a part of the program. (Incidentally, school staff participants didn't have to be teachers; some of our strongest presenters were custodial and security staff members.)

At our Power Monday meetings, we discussed a wide range of topics that are vitally important to our black male students' growth and development—entrepreneurship, goal setting, leadership, parenting, relationships, community development, and more.

We discussed many topics not only from the vantage point of the present but also from the vantage point of ten to twenty years in the future. Far too many inner-city African American black males said they cannot see themselves living beyond the age of twenty-one. I wanted to change this kind of thinking and to help our students develop a vision for their lives.

When we discussed parenting, for example, we encouraged students to start thinking about their own future roles as parents even though they were only in middle. We were planting seeds for the future. We were also building on the past as we introduced our black male students to the history of our people.

This was vital because so many of them were unaware that they were the descendants of greatness. As Professor Maulana Karenga (1982), the creator of Kwanzaa, wrote, "History gives blacks an understanding of themselves by suggesting possibilities of future national and world achievement based on what they have achieved in the past (p. 49)." Our Power Monday meetings were stimulating, and the students looked forward to them every week. The young men particularly liked the diversity of speakers. Men from all walks of life from professional men to those recently released from prison were guest speakers who shared personal stories that empowered our students.

The successful men shared what they did to get to where they were, including mistakes they had made and overcome; the men coming out of prison shared how their failure to take education seriously put them on a path of poor decision-making and incarceration.

Another effective aspect of Power Monday meetings was having our black male students address topics and questions from the lectern, thus helping them learn how to speak publicly and think on their feet. Typically, each grade level would meet once a month. Periodically, I would convene a Power Monday meeting of the school's entire male population, in which the older students would often take the lead by offering advice and suggestions to their younger peers. This not only enabled the younger students to learn from their older peers but also built accountability for the older students who felt obligated to be a positive role model for the younger students.

What were the results of my program? Right before my eyes, I witnessed growth and change. My African American male students were evolving. They were transforming! They were maturing! They were conducting themselves as mature young black leaders of the future.

Why Keep Your Son Out of Special Education if He Is Not Disabled?

There are many reasons why you should keep your son out of special education if he does not have a learning disability. I want to mention three in particular: Your son may carry a lasting stigma from receiving special education that could be injurious to his reputation and long-term educational and social prospects.

What's more, he may suffer irreversible intellectual damage from being in special education since many teachers continue to expect very little from disabled students. And once your son has been placed in special education, it can be difficult to transfer him out even if subsequent evaluations show that he does not require it. In one of my classes, there was a student named Zion (not his real name). He had great difficulty comprehending very simple concepts. Repeating the simplest concepts a hundred different ways did not help him comprehend them. Everyone assumed, therefore, that he was severely disabled.

No one was certain that he was disabled, but it was obvious that something was severely wrong with her comprehension. For Zion and others like him, special education is a noble and beneficial idea. When it works, it provides disabled students with the special learning environments and resources they need without cramping the learning styles of their peers.

When schools place truly disabled students in special education, they are helping those students obtain a FAPE. That we should applaud. On the other hand, it is appalling and a grave injustice when schools place nondisabled African American males in special education merely on the basis of race.

We should condemn and repudiate this discriminatory practice soundly given the gravity of this injustice on African Americans, their families, and their future. The result of such disproportionate placement is a gross overrepresentation of black students, especially black males, in special education, and a gross underrepresentation of black students, especially black males, in gifted education.

The problem with African American males is that special education is very bad according to recent reports released by the Office for Civil Rights (OCR) of the United States Department of Education. During the 2019–2019 school year, the OCR reports that black students comprised only 14.4 percent of the total student population, but 19 percent of the 6,086,426 students were served under IDEA. Regarding African American males, in particular, they represented 12.8 percent of the 4,057,058 male students served under IDEA.

Incidentally, the percentage of blacks in special education in many confederate states greatly exceeded the national average of 14.4 percent. For example, blacks comprise 40 percent of the special education population in Alabama, 39.4 percent in Georgia, 50 percent in Louisiana, 52.4 percent in Mississippi, 43 percent in South Carolina, and 45.2 percent in Maryland. Given the legacy of white supremacy in southern states, this fact is unsurprising. In another revealing report, the United States Department of Education stated that black students were overrepresented in all thirteen disability categories. The population of blacks in two of those categories (mental retardation and developmentally delayed) represented twice their proportion of the school population. What's more, when black students are placed in special education, they are more likely than white students to be put in highly restrictive environments where little real education takes place.

Lastly, the report showed that black students ages six through twenty-one were 1.4 times more likely of receiving special education services than all other racial/ethnic groups combined.

Special education classes have changed drastically in the past twenty years; namely, the students who take advantage of these adapted learning classrooms have changed. Contemporary public school education recognizes that there are degrees of disabilities that may impact student learning, and the rise of conditions like autism has fueled the need for more special education intervention.

As a result, the mental image that even today's youngest educators have of special education students is probably not accurate. For example, did you know that African American males are more likely than any other group to be placed in special education classes, with

80 percent of all special education students being black or Hispanic males? African American males account for 20 percent of United States students labeled as mentally retarded, even though they represent just 9 percent of the population. On the other end of the extreme, black boys are 2.5 times less likely to be classified as "gifted and talented" even if their academic record shows that potential.

If all things were weighed equally, these statistics would indicate that there is something genetically wrong with these African American males that are causing a higher incidence of disabilities and a smaller percentage of gifted individuals. Educators know better. While some, perhaps even a majority, of the black boys categorized as special education students belong in that grouping, some are simply misunderstood. While unpleasant behavior is certainly a symptom of learning disabilities—like ADHD and some degrees of autism—it isn't in and of itself a disability.

A lack of understanding surrounding how black boys interact with the world and a quick trigger when it comes to disciplinary and removal practices is contributing to higher-than-average numbers of black boys in special education classrooms. This is not something that any educator can sit by and continue, for it impacts the way all students are treated in the public school landscape.

Every student I was privileged to teach knew they have an advocate. No matter what race they were, I fought for their rights. They become vulnerable and transparent, allowing me to instill knowledge and empower them holistically. Together, we were resilient: breaking down barriers, combating stereotypes, and reaching new levels of success in life, on the football field, basketball court, and in the classroom.

African American Male Role Models

This vision did not start with me. During the month of February, when I reflected on our country's most inspiring black leaders, I knew I am a part of a much larger mission that began long ago. It truly takes a village to achieve the long-term solutions needed to overcome systemic barriers that disproportionately hinder African

American males' access to the educational opportunity that allows them to build the future of their choosing. Throughout my twenty-year career as an inner-city special education teacher and mentor, I am part of a diverse network of leaders committed to changing this reality. I'm addressing an urgent opportunity to change the way African American male students see themselves and guide them toward new possibilities for their futures. With my story, example, and purpose, I am building more success stories along the way.

The School-to-Prison Pipeline

African American males disproportionately lack access to the kind of education that can open the doors to a world of opportunity. In Meridian, Mississippi, police routinely arrest and transport African American males to a juvenile detention center for minor classroom misbehaviors.

In Jefferson Parish, Los Angeles, according to a United States Department of Justice complaint, school officials have given armed police "unfettered authority to stop, frisk, detain, question, search and arrest schoolchildren on and off school grounds." In Birmingham, Alabama, police officers are permanently stationed in nearly every high school.

In fact, hundreds of school districts across the country employ discipline policies that push African American males out of the classroom and into the criminal justice system at alarming rates—a phenomenon known as the school-to-prison pipeline. Senator Richard Durbin, D-Ill, held the first federal hearing on the school-to-prison pipeline—an important step toward ending policies that favor incarceration over education and disproportionately push minority students and students with disabilities out of schools and into jails.

In opening the hearing, Durbin told the subcommittee of the Senate Judiciary Committee, "For many young people, our schools are increasingly a gateway to the criminal justice system specially African American males. This phenomenon is a consequence of a culture of zero tolerance that is widespread in our schools and is depriving many children of their fundamental right to an education."

A wide array of organizations—including the Southern Poverty Law Center, the NAACP, and Dignity in Schools—testified during the hearing.

They joined representatives from the Departments of Education and Justice to shine a national spotlight on a situation viewed far too often as a local responsibility. "We have a national problem that deserves federal action," Matthew Cregor, an attorney with the NAACP Legal Defense Fund, explained. "With suspension a top predictor of dropout, we must confront this practice if we are ever to end the 'dropout crisis' or the so-called achievement gap." In the words of Vermont's Senator Patrick Leahy, "As a nation, we can do better." The United State must do better for out African American males.

What is the school-to-prison pipeline?

Policies that encourage police presence at schools, harsh tactics including physical restraint, and automatic punishments that result in suspensions and out-of-class time are huge contributors to the pipeline, but the problem is more complex than that.

The school-to-prison pipeline starts in the classroom. When combined with zero-tolerance policies, a teacher's decision to refer students for punishment can mean they are pushed out of the classroom—and much more likely to be introduced into the criminal justice system.

Who's in the pipeline?

African American males and males of color make up this pipeline. These students from two groups' racial minorities and children with disabilities are disproportionately represented in the school-to-prison pipeline. African American students, for instance, are 3.5 times more likely than their white classmates to be suspended or expelled, according to a nationwide study by the United States Department of Education Office for Civil Rights.

Black children constitute 18 percent of students, but they account for 46 percent of those suspended more than once. For students with disabilities, the numbers are equally troubling. One report found that while 8.6 percent of public school children have been identified as having disabilities that affect their ability to learn, these students make up 32 percent of youth in juvenile detention centers.

The racial disparities are even starker for students with disabilities. About one in four black children with disabilities are suspended at least once versus one in eleven white students according to an analysis of the government report by Daniel J. Losen, director of the Center for Civil Rights Remedies of the Civil Rights Project at UCLA. A landmark study published last year tracked nearly one million Texas students for at least six years. The study controlled for more than eighty variables, such as socioeconomic class, to see how they affected the likelihood of school discipline.

The study found that African Americans, especially males, were disproportionately punished compared with otherwise similar white and Latino students. Children with emotional disabilities also were disproportionately suspended and expelled. In other studies, Losen found racial differences in suspension rates have widened since the early 1970s and that suspension is being used more frequently as a disciplinary tool for African American males who look like me. But Losen said his recent study and other research show that removing children from school does not improve their behavior. Instead, it greatly increases the likelihood that they'll drop out and wind up behind bars.

Punishing policies

The SPLC advocates for changes to end the school-to-prison pipeline and has filed lawsuits or civil rights complaints against districts with punitive discipline practices that are discriminatory in impact. According to the United States Department of Justice, the number of school resource officers rose 38 percent between 1997 and 2007. Jerri Katzerman, SPLC deputy legal director, said this surge in police on campus has helped to criminalize many African American male students and fill the pipeline. One study found that African American males are far more likely to be arrested at school than they were a generation ago.

The vast majority of these arrests are for nonviolent offenses. In most cases, the students are simply being disruptive. And a recent United States Department of Education study found that more than 70 percent of students arrested in school-related incidents or referred to law enforcement are black or Hispanic. Zero-tolerance policies, which set one-size-fits-all punishments for a variety of behaviors, have fed these trends.

Best practices

Instead of pushing children out, teachers need a lot more support and training for effective discipline, and schools need to use best practices for behavior modification to keep African American males and males of color in schools where they belong. I know from twenty years of teaching that keeping at-risk kids in the class can be a tough order for educators under pressure to meet accountability measures, but classroom teachers are in a unique position to divert students from the school-to-prison pipeline.

Teachers know their students better than any resource officer or administrator—which puts them in a singularly empowered position to keep students in the classroom. It's not easy, but when teachers take a more responsive and less punitive approach in the classroom, students are more likely to complete their education. I can say this because I have seen it happen in my classroom.

The information in "A Teacher's Guide to Rerouting the Pipeline" highlights common scenarios that push young people into the school-to-prison pipeline and offers practical advice for how teachers can dismantle the school-to-prison pipeline. I firmly believe that school districts across America can help to divert this school-to-prison pipeline. In our present-day society, it's a fight that many are losing; however, as an African American male special education teacher, I will continue to fight to keep black or brown males out of a system that has been set up against them.

Avoiding the pipeline

How can school districts divert the school-to-prison pipeline?

- Increase the use of positive behavior interventions and supports.
- Compile annual reports on the total number of disciplinary actions that push students out of the classroom based on gender, race, and ability.
- Create agreements with police departments and court systems to limit arrests at school and the use of restraints, such as mace and handcuffs.
- Provide simple explanations of infractions and prescribed responses in the student code of conduct to ensure fairness.
- Expand the program.

As a result of the success of these empowerment meetings, I developed a comprehensive model for a Young Men's Empowerment Program for elementary and middle school African American males of color. In addition to Power Monday assemblies, here are some additional components that may be included in such a program:

- Small-group sessions of three to ten students led by African American men.
- One-to-one mentoring with an African American male for individual males who especially need guidance
- Opportunities to meet and spend time with African American male college students, including visits to a college campus
- Opportunities to meet and spend time with successful black men in their work environment through partnerships with specific companies and agencies
- Having African American males in positions of political leadership meet with students at the school, as well as allowing students to visit them in their local offices

- Dressing for success days. If it is not practical to have all students dress professionally every Monday, as we did in my school, you can set aside special dress-for-success days and treat them as celebrations.
- After-school male study groups, in which students with specific interests discuss those interests—for example, learning about black historical figures, such as Malcolm X, George Washington Carver, Dr. Martin Luther King, and Frederick Douglass.

A universal message

Although there are many strategies that good teachers of any gender and ethnicity can implement on a classroom level to support the success of black male students, I believe that to maximize our classroom efforts, we must ensure that young black males have opportunities to learn from role models whom they can identify with. The best way of making this happen is to launch a Young Men's Empowerment Program, rooted in Power Mondays (which can actually occur any day of the week). The program works as effectively in racially diverse schools as it does in majority-black schools. The message of self-respect is universal, so all students can benefit.

The Tuskegee of the North

For over half a century, this four-hundred-acre estate was home to the New Jersey Manual Training and Industrial School for Colored Youth, also known as the Bordentown School. Originally founded in 1886 by the formerly enslaved Reverend Walter Rice as an industrial school for Black girls, the school ultimately became an elite coed, state-run boarding school for New Jersey's black students. Recognized as the "Tuskegee of the North" after Booker T. Washington's Tuskegee Institute in Alabama, the Bordentown School developed a reputation for preparing its African American students for a lifetime of leadership through vocational training and academic studies. Empowered by this education, graduates of the school enjoyed successful careers in fields such as law, medicine, education, and skilled trades.

Tuskegee of the North, as it was known, also attracted visits from such luminaries as Mary McLeod Bethune, W. E. B. Du Bois, Booker T. Washington, Nat King Cole, Duke Ellington, Albert Einstein, Eleanor Roosevelt, and Paul Robeson, among others. But in 1947, New Jersey adopted a state constitutional provision that prohibited public school segregation and required the Bordentown School to integrate the following year. After the school attracted only two white students, New Jersey closed the Bordentown School in 1955, just one year after the Supreme Court's decision in Brown v. Board of Education, arguing that it perpetuated racial segregation. More than sixty years after, New Jersey closed the Bordentown School's (Tuskegee of the North) doors. Most of its many campus buildings are uninhabitable and abandoned, yet some remain in use. So what now occupies the land that was once home to the "Tuskegee of the North?" New Jersey's only girls' youth prison—the Female Secure Care and Intake Facility, also known as Hayes. New Jersey's failed experiment with youth incarceration, which has devastated the lives of black youth, is the inverse of the Bordentown School (the institution that uplifted black youth).

New Jersey has the worst racial disparities among its incarcerated black and white youth in the nation. In New Jersey, a black child is over thirty times more likely to be detained or committed to a youth facility than a white child. As a result, as of June 1, 2017, 70 percent of incarcerated kids are black, and only 8 percent (just eighteen kids) are white. Of the twelve girls in prison at Hayes, the majority (75 percent) are black.

Racial disparities and the closure of the Bordentown School and its replacement with a youth prison are vivid representations of how the prison house has replaced the schoolhouse for too many African American males in our state. As of June 1, 2017, there are 232 youth incarcerated in New Jersey's three youth prisons. Of this number, 163 are black, and only eighteen are white. Even more glaring, only two white youth, out of a total of sixty-five young people, were housed in JMSF—the same number of white students who attended the Bordentown School after integration. These striking disparities persist even though research shows that black and white youth commit most offenses at similar rates.

Fact 1

Can I really tell you the naked truth?

Troubling truths about black boys and the United States educational system

Most people like to think that American K–12 schools, workplaces, and courthouses are pillars of fairness but, statistic after statistic, all point to a crisis among the African American males of the nation. This crisis begins in homes, stretches to K–12 educational experiences, and leads straight to the cycle of incarceration in increasingly high numbers. In America's prison systems, black citizens are incarcerated six times the rates of white ones, and the NAACP predicts that one in three of this generation of African black men will spend some time locked up.

Bring Our Children Home

A prime example of the prison-to-school pipeline for New Jersey's African American youth details the Bordentown campus' transformation from school to prison, as well as the modern-day devastating impact of the school-to-prison pipeline on New Jersey's youth of color.

"It is imperative that we rebuild our justice system to be transformative and prioritize rehabilitation," Congresswoman Bonnie Watson Coleman said. "The solutions to reform our criminal justice system must begin with affirming and preserving the humanity of African American our children."

"Our new youth justice system must begin to correct the inequities and heal the pain felt by families of color who have been victimized by the youth justice system," Assemblywoman Mila Jasey added. "Black children in New Jersey are over 30 times more likely than their white peers to be detained or committed, even though black and white children commit most offenses at similar rates. These shameful disparities exist and persist because of racially discriminatory policy decisions that disproportionately impact African American children."

Institute Associate Counsel Andrea McChristian released her report Bring Our Children Home:

The Tuskegee of the North

For more than fifty years, New Jersey ran the Bordentown School, an elite public boarding school for African American youth. Known as the "Tuskegee of the North," the school attracted visits from luminaries like W.E.B. DuBois, Duke Ellington, Albert Einstein, and Paul Robeson. However, the campus became the home to the Female Secure Care and Intake Facility, known as Hayes, New Jersey's only youth prison for girls.

"The Bordentown campus, once a pinnacle of black uplift, became the home to Hayes, New Jersey's only youth prison for girls. And across the street sits the Juvenile Medium Security Facility, New Jersey's most secure youth prison for boys," said Ryan P. Haygood, Institute President and CEO. "Bordentown is, literally, the school to prison pipeline realized."

According to the Institute's report's findings:

During the 2013–2014 school years, black students, who made up about 16% of total enrollment in New Jersey, made up an estimated 35.3% of students receiving one or more in-school suspensions, 43.7% of students receiving one or more out-of-school suspensions, and 37% of students receiving expulsions with or without educational services. Black students in the state also made up an estimated 34.5% of school-related arrests and 31.4% of referrals to law enforcement.

Over the 2013–2014 school year, while black girls made up only 16.2% of female students in New Jersey, they made up an estimated half (50.4%) of girls receiving one or more out-of-school suspensions, 30.2% of girls receiving expulsions with or without educational services, 37.6% of girls subject to school related arrests, and 33.9% of girls referred to law enforcement.

As of June 1, 2017, there are 232 youth incarcerated in New Jersey's three youth prisons. Of this number, 163 are black and only eighteen are white. Of the twelve girls in prison at Hayes, the majority (75%) are black.

"These racial disparities do not reflect greater culpability of black children than their white peers, as black and white youth commit most offenses at similar rates," said primary author and Institute Associate Counsel Andrea McChristian. "Rather, these disparities exist, in part, because of our schools' inability to see black children as children. Our new youth justice system must view all children as children, and provide them with the grace, compassion, and support they need."

Conduct a qualitative study of the school-to-prison pipeline. The New Jersey Department of Education should conduct a statewide, comprehensive school-to-prison pipeline qualitative study. The research should include focus groups and interviews with students, families, teachers, school law enforcers, guidance counselors, social workers, nurses, administrators, and others involved with school environments and should primarily target school districts with high rates of suspensions, expulsions, law enforcement referrals, and arrests.

"If we truly want to end the school-to-prison pipeline in this state and around the country, we must take the recommendations offered seriously and inject these ideas into every aspect of how we discuss, design, and implement educational policies and reform," Dr. Lauren Wells said, who specializes in public education and designing education to cultivate and nurture the intellect, talent, and self-determination of black and brown children.

Importantly, these racial disparities do not reflect the greater culpability of black children than their white peers as black and white youth commit most offenses at similar rates. Rather, these disparities exist, in part, because of our schools' inability to see black children as children. Indeed, both black boys and girls are seen as less innocent and more mature than their white peers. Studies also show the implicit bias some educators have toward viewing black youth as more likely to engage in disruptive behavior even among students as young as preschool age.

The United States Department of Education Office for Civil Rights recognized this issue, affirming that "racial discrimination in school discipline is a real problem" after identifying instances of schools disciplining black students more harshly and more frequently because of their race than similarly situated white students. On this note, given that New Jersey has some of the most racially segregated schools in the nation, an important area for further research in our state is the overlap of school racial segregation and punitive disciplinary measures.

School-to-Prison Pipeline Continues

The ACLU is committed to challenging the "school-to-prison pipeline," a disturbing national trend wherein children are funneled out of public schools and into the juvenile and criminal justice systems. Many of these children have learning disabilities or histories of poverty, abuse, or neglect and would benefit from additional educational and counseling services. Instead, they are isolated, punished, and pushed out.

"Zero-tolerance" policies criminalize minor infractions of school rules, while cops in schools lead to students being criminalized for behavior that should be handled inside the school. Students of color are especially vulnerable to push-out trends and the discriminatory application of discipline.

Related Resources

The ACLU believes that children should be educated, not incarcerated. We are working to challenge numerous policies and practices within public school systems and the juvenile justice system that contribute to the school-to-prison pipeline.

For a growing number of students, the path to incarceration includes the "stops" below.

Failing Public Schools

For most students, the pipeline begins with *inadequate resources in public schools*. Overcrowded classrooms, a lack of qualified teachers, and insufficient funding for "extras" such as counselors, special education services, and even textbooks, lock students into second-rate educational environments. This failure to meet educational needs increases disengagement and dropouts, increasing the risk of later court involvement. Even worse, schools may actually encourage dropouts in response to pressures from test-based accountability regimes such as the No Child Left Behind Act, which create incentives to push out low-performing students to boost overall test scores.

Zero-Tolerance and Other School Discipline

Lacking resources, facing incentives to push out low-performing students, and responding to a handful of highly publicized school shootings, schools have embraced ***zero-tolerance policies*** that automatically impose severe punishment regardless of circumstances. Under these policies, students have been expelled for bringing nail clippers or scissors to school. Rates of ***suspension*** have increased dramatically in recent years—from 1.7 million in 1974 to 3.1 million in 2000 (3)—and have been most dramatic for children of color.

Overly harsh disciplinary policies push students down the pipeline and into the juvenile justice system. Suspended and expelled children are often left unsupervised and without constructive activities; they also can easily fall behind in their coursework, leading to a greater likelihood of disengagement and drop-outs. All of these factors increase the likelihood of court involvement. (4)

As harsh penalties for minor misbehavior become more pervasive, ***schools increasingly ignore or bypass due process protections*** for suspensions and expulsions. The lack of due process is particularly acute for ***students with special needs***, who are disproportionately represented in the pipeline despite the heightened protections afforded to them under law.

Policing School Hallways

Many under-resourced schools become pipeline gateways by placing ***increased reliance***

on police rather than teachers and administrators to maintain discipline. Growing numbers of districts employ ***school resource officers*** to patrol school hallways, often with little or no training in working with youth. As a result, children are far more likely to be subject to ***school-based arrests***—the majority of which are for non-violent offenses, such as disruptive behavior—than they were a generation ago. The rise in school-based arrests, the quickest route from the classroom to the jailhouse, most directly exemplifies the criminalization of school children.

Disciplinary Alternative Schools

In some jurisdictions, students who have been suspended or expelled have no right to an education at all. In others, they are sent to ***disciplinary alternative schools***.

Growing in number across the country, these shadow systems—sometimes run by private, for-profit companies—are immune from educational accountability standards (such as minimum classroom hours and curriculum requirements) and may fail to provide meaningful educational services to the students who need them the most. As a result, struggling students return to their regular schools unprepared, are permanently locked into inferior educational settings, or are funneled through alternative schools into the juvenile justice system.

Court Involvement and Juvenile Detention

Youth who become involved in the juvenile justice system are often denied procedural protections in the courts; in one state, up to 80% of court-involved children do not have lawyers.

(5) Students who commit minor offenses may end up in secured detention if they violate boilerplate probation conditions prohibiting them from activities like missing school or disobeying teachers.

Students pushed along the pipeline find themselves in *juvenile detention facilities*, many of which provide few, if any, educational services. Students of color—who are far more likely than their white peers to be suspended, expelled, or arrested for the *same kind* of conduct at school (6)—and those with disabilities are particularly likely to travel down this pipeline. (7)

Though many students are propelled down the pipeline from school to jail, it is difficult for them to make the journey in reverse. Students who enter the juvenile justice system face many **barriers to their re-entry** into traditional schools. The vast majority of these students never graduate from high school.

Experts describe the school-to-prison pipeline as the result of practices that force students out of the classroom and into the justice system. Students in hundreds of school districts nationally are susceptible to zero-tolerance policies and denied education for often minor misbehaviors. Alarmingly, students of color and students with special needs are disciplined at disproportionate rates compared to the greater student population.

This is especially problematic given that schools over-rely on police forces to maintain on-campus discipline, leading to student arrests. With the abuses of power and significant racial disparities seen in prosecution and detention, the school-to-prison pipeline is a continuation of the most broken parts of America's justice system. And yet, there is no evidence to support the efficacy of these forms of discipline. Claims that zero-tolerance policies are an effective approach to controlling classrooms and helping students become healthy, well-adjusted members of society fail to hold up in light of data. Instead, such policies drive students into the justice system, creating a dangerous cycle that deprives youth of meaningful opportunities for education, future employment, and success.

What is zero tolerance?

Zero-tolerance policies require school administrators to suspend or expel students for misconduct, regardless of the severity, circumstances, or context of the situation. No single definition exists across the American educational system, making outcomes difficult to track and compare, but such policies are prevalent throughout the nation and in New Jersey.

Punishments often manifest as referrals to the youth justice system—the foundation of the school-to-prison pipeline.

Origins of zero tolerance

The now-debunked "broken windows" theory, introduced in 1982, suggested that "crime is a disorder that, if not eliminated or controlled early on, increases [a person's] likelihood of committing a more serious crime later in life." The theory was based on the idea that a broken window in a neighborhood would encourage further vandalism or disorder—meaning police should focus on punishment for minor misconduct to prevent more significant infractions. The application of the theory led to an increase in arrests for nonviolent crimes, such as panhandling, disorderly conduct, and public intoxication. In schools, the ideas undergirding the theory led to harsher punishments for common misconduct.

In 1994, the Gun-Free Schools Act (GFSA) inspired school districts to write zero-tolerance policies into their code. The GFSA mandated that states whose schools receive federal funding must expel for at least one year any student found to have brought a firearm to school.

In 1994, former President Bill Clinton established the Office of Community Oriented Policing Services (COPS) in the Department of Justice; since its implementation, it has become the largest contributor to increased police forces in schools, with three hundred million dollars allocated for school policing alone. In the midst of expansions of manpower for school policing, schools were given agency to expand zero-tolerance policies to fit other types of misconduct.

Terms such as *willful defiance* were included as suspendable offenses. This encompassed a wide range of subjective *offenses*, from dress code violations to *horseplay*. Chapter 37 of the Texas Education Code outlines policies for school "discipline, law and order" and is largely based on the Texas Penal Code (change this to new)—effectively creating an education system that mirrors a justice system inappropriate for children. And, as noted above, there has been no evidence that suspensions and expulsions are an effective method of changing students' behavior in schools.

Disparities in the application of zero tolerance

Students of color, students with special needs, young boys, and children in foster care are consistently overrepresented in suspension and expulsion rates compared to the larger student population. The latest civil rights data from the United States Department of Education shows that black preschoolers comprised 18 percent of preschool enrollment but received 48 percent of out-of-school suspensions. Black students comprised 15 percent of the overall school population but received 39 percent of out-of-school suspensions. Black males comprised approximately 8 percent of the entire student population but received 25 percent of out-of-school suspensions and 23 percent of expulsions. Black females similarly comprised approximately 8 percent of the student population but received 14 percent of suspensions.

The rates of out-of-school suspension are similar for Latinx students, with males representing 13 percent of the student population but receiving 15 percent of suspensions. Students with special needs who are served by the Individuals with Disabilities Education Act (IDEA) are more than twice as likely to receive one or more out-of-school suspensions as other students. In Texas, the rates of disparity are no different. While black students comprised 13 percent of the student population from 2017 to 2018, they represented 33 percent of all out-of-school suspensions and 25 percent of all in-school suspensions. Similarly, students with disabilities comprised only 10 percent of the Texas student population but accounted for 20 percent of all out-of-school suspensions, 16 percent of in-school suspensions, and 17 percent of referrals to disciplinary alternative education programs.

This tragic overrepresentation of certain students in disciplinary actions is seen in referrals to law enforcement and arrests as well. Black students, who comprise 15 percent of student enrollment nationally, represent 31 percent of students referred to law enforcement or arrested. Students with special needs represent a quarter of the students who are referred to law enforcement or subjected to school-related arrests but comprise just 12 percent of the student population. Very young children are a large portion of students represented in these statistics. From 2015 to 2016 in Texas alone, 63,874 children from prekindergarten through fifth grade received an out-of-school suspension; 144,432 children were removed from the classroom and placed into in-school suspension. From 2017 to 2018, children in foster care from prekindergarten to second grade in the state of Texas were three times more likely than their peers to be suspended.

Harsh disciplinary practices for very young children are harmful for a number of reasons:

Expulsion and suspension for young children lead to high rates of expulsion and suspension later in school. Labeling young children (as ones warranting harsh discipline) has lasting detrimental effects on their social-emotional learning; it also creates a negative lens through which teachers and administrators view students from year to year.

Negative impacts on social-emotional learning in kindergarten have been shown to create negative outcomes in many areas, such as future unemployment, criminal activity, substance use, and mental and physical health issues.

Policymakers in some states have taken action. After a report on California schools found that 15 percent of elementary school suspensions and 21 percent of middle school suspensions were for "willful defiance," and that black males were being suspended four times the student average, California banned suspensions for "willful defiance" by students in kindergarten through eighth grade.

In 2017, the Texas Legislature passed House Bill 674, banning discretionary out-of-school suspensions and expulsions for students in kindergarten through second grade. Unfortunately, due to limited oversight of the bill's provisions, very young children have continued to be suspended and expelled at alarming rates. Also problematic, a 2014 federal school discipline policy that urged schools to only suspend, expel, or report students to police as a last resort was overturned in December 2018 under the Trump administration. Professionals assert that disparities in the application of zero tolerance are the result of systematic failures in the education system.

For instance, a lack of support for teachers and administrators (including funding, additional personnel, and training and professional development) creates an overreliance on traditional discipline. Other drivers of disparities in the application of zero tolerance include the following:

Lack of trauma-informed care

Students experiencing trauma may have a variety of symptoms that impact their experience in the classroom and prevent them from successfully managing stress or other emotions. For instance, students in foster care are more likely than their counterparts to have experienced adverse childhood experiences. The trauma associated with these experiences may cause behaviors that lead to discipline or suspension. Similarly, children with special needs may experience struggles in the classroom, leading to outbursts that result in them being removed from class.

Labeling

In part due to teachers' lack of access to consistent, relevant training and proper resources, they may be unable to help high-needs students and instead may label them as "troublemakers" or "problem students." These labels can stay with children who adopt them as personal narratives, and they are especially problematic when communicated to a student's future teacher. This standard of labeling effectively severs students' connectedness to their learning environments and their relationships with staff and their peers and can create a cycle of disciplinary actions.

WHAT IS RESTORATIVE JUSTICE?

Dr. Philip Carney, the Restorative Discipline Coordinator at North East Independent School District in San Antonio, Texas, shared this.

Restorative justice is a disciplinary practice that seeks to repair harm by addressing the root cause of the actor's conduct, ultimately mitigating the likelihood of their behavior recurring. Using methods such as group conferencing, healing circles, check-ins, and mediated victim offender dialogue (VOD), restorative justice helps the actor consider the consequences of their actions; it also encourages empathy by using age-appropriate, feeling-centered language. In the school setting, restorative justice involves not only the misbehaving student, but the person harmed and the community around them. Including the community fosters a feeling of responsibility for the student, thereby strengthening and uniting a community around their young people. In schools, restorative justice serves as a disciplinary practice and a learning opportunity. When compared to traditional disciplinary methods, restorative justice requires high levels of accountability from students.

Dr. Philip Carney said professionals and students, he spoke with, repeatedly emphasized that while restorative justice is the age-appropriate response, it is not a soft approach to discipline. In requiring varying levels of participation and engagement both in proactive and reactive actions, building and maintaining a restorative culture requires much of students, most of all from the student who caused harm. From the requirement of taking responsibility for the wrongdoing, to making a sincere apology, to developing a plan for restitution satisfactory to the victim, to ultimately following through on that plan, professionals and students agree far more accountability is required of a student making amends through a restorative justice model than one who is sent home via suspension or expulsion.

The roots of restorative justice are in the community healing practices of multiple indigenous groups. Ramon Vasquez, Male Outreach Coordinator at American Indians in Texas at the Spanish Colonial Missions, shared the importance of remembering the roots of practices that have only in recent years come to be known as restorative justice. Drawing on historical accounts of Native American conflict resolution methods, while war was certainly an aspect of pre-colonized America, many Native American tribes sought peace and utilized violence only as a last resort. Similar practices have historically been employed by other groups as well, from the New Zealand Maori restorative system to the African ubuntu system. The work of these groups has been focused on community repair rather than retribution. According to Mr. Vasquez, "It is a colonized thought that war is the way to resolve conflict." He parallels the historic concepts to today's work in schools, stating, "If we're modeling to our children that violence [via a police force] is the way to establish control, how can we expect kids to do things differently?"

While many restorative justice programs in United States schools are still in the early stages of implementation, the outcomes have been overwhelmingly positive, with many empirical studies showing a decrease in exclusionary discipline and harmful behavior following implementation.

Qualitatively, the benefits of restorative justice are numerous: Dr. Anita Wadwha, Dean of Students at Yes Prep Northbrook High School in Houston, Texas, asserts that, because misbehaving students have a voice in the disciplinary process, they experience an increased sense of control, providing that sense of ownership helps eliminate the feeling of helplessness that can contribute to further misconduct. Additionally, involving the person harmed, as well as the community, in the restorative justice process encourages accountability by showing misbehaving students that their actions affect those around them, while still giving them ample opportunity to redeem themselves. Restorative justice methods isolate and confront the harmful behavior, rather than the students themselves, which helps the students feel safe as they work to understand the underlying cause of their behavior and fix the issue.

Restorative justice methods also help students become more empathetic with their community, which improves pro-social behaviors overall, leading to a decrease in harmful behaviors and lowered recidivism rates. Victims are provided a safe, facilitated environment where they can express the depth of the harm they have experienced, and where the student who caused harm acknowledges and validates the experience of the victim.

Together, they work to develop a plan to address the harm in a way that serves and empowers the victim directly. This results in the victim feeling a sense of justice while still creating a distinction between the isolated behavior and the student responsible. Victims also experience greater healing as they feel a renewed sense of safety in their community and as they experience less victimization overall.

Restorative justice benefits the community, providing a more efficient and cost-effective means of reparation compared to the youth justice system. Furthermore, through restorative justice programs, students who have caused harm are given the opportunity to serve and interact with their communities, creating an equitable and mutually beneficial relationship, which greatly aids the student's reintegration process. And, as mentioned above, restorative justice programs produce lower recidivism rates, leading to greater public safety.

Dr. Wadhwa, as the coordinator behind the six-year restorative justice program at Northbrook High School, is one of the top experts on restorative justice models in Texas. Dr. Wadhwa implements a restorative justice program based on the Youth Apprenticeship

Model (YAM). YAM promotes youth leadership, training youth to facilitate restorative circles and to train other youth. The goal of the program is to empower youth to transform themselves, their relationships, and the school system as a whole. Every student at Yes Prep attends restorative circles once a week. This allows students to build a community by getting to know each other and becoming more comfortable expressing themselves. Students interested in facilitating restorative circles can apply to enroll in the leadership class where they are taught the principles and benefits of restorative justice and trained to conduct circles.

During the restorative circles, three questions are asked:

1. What happened?
2. What was the impact?
3. What will be done to make it right?

All participants are given the opportunity to speak, share their feelings, and be part of the solution. Healing circles are the first and primary intervention used, rather than disciplinary referrals to school administration. In the event that a restorative circle is unsuccessful in holding a student accountable, the traditional disciplinary route is sought. When students were asked why they prefer restorative circles, the resounding responses were "you get to speak your truth" and "you can have your voice heard." Students appreciate that circles provide a space for understanding, something that is not possible when students are removed from their peers rather than engaging in conversations to repair the harm caused.

When asked about alternative discipline methods—such as restorative justice—as a replacement for school policing, Dr. Wadhwa said,

> It's all discipline. Restorative justice is all about helping kids by creating accountability. It allows kids to take control of their lives and their own education. It's simply about punitive versus restorative, levels of control versus levels

of support in the models. The traditional model tends to be punitive with low levels of support and high-level disciplines. But with staffing and capacity, we can make every space a restorative space. Basic things take a lot of work for adults, so discipline has to be youth-led. (Sizemore 1988, Murphy and Hallinger 1998)

Fixing the Leaky Classroom Pipeline

For African American male teachers, underrepresentation continues to plague those who seek to increase the presence of black males in classrooms across the nation. Our research found that black male teachers often note similarities within their experiences once entering school settings. Overall, African American teachers are often recruited to teach in schools serving large populations of students of color, many *plagued with a lack of resources* and high teacher turnover rates.

Those who become teachers often face difficulties with teacher preparation programs that frequently become barriers to teacher certification. In addition, they face challenges with standardized testing, instances of racism, marginalization, and isolation, all of which often have serious implications.

Taking action

Increasing the black male teacher representation in schools across the nation requires strategic planning, including collaborative efforts at the national, state, district, and local levels. A long-term commitment of resources and continuous championing for diversity of our nation's classrooms remains the most promising way to effectively staff schools with black male educators.

To combat obstacles around recruiting, retaining, and advancing black male educators, there is an obligation for policymakers and school administrators to examine and implement sustainable initiatives aimed at creating inclusive, equitable, and supportive school environments where all can thrive.

The voice of African American males

Diversifying our nation's classrooms. Black male students benefit from having a black male teacher, with research noting lower dropout rates, fewer disciplinary issues, more positive views of schooling, and better test scores

The voices of these African American male educators demonstrate that a diverse and inclusive workforce within PK–12 education is critical to ensuring that our nation's students receive a robust, quality education. J. Medgar Roberts was an author of the paper and NNSTOY contributor. His story is a great example of the impact of diversity in today's classrooms.

A year into his teaching career, Roberts found himself the sole African American male core content teacher at his school after a legendary career math teacher retired. He would soon learn that this was a trend in many schools. In his twenty-five years teaching middle and high school, the most black male colleagues he's worked with were around fifteen—out of a staff of more than three hundred. And that number is highly unusual.

A special story recently emerged regarding Roberts. After changing schools and moving more than 150 miles away, a former student—a young black male graduate of the class of 2019 whom Roberts never taught in the classroom—thanked him for his mentorship and support during convocation. The young man is an aspiring educator, and Roberts was the teacher at the school who understood his situation. Though he did not intentionally enter the role of mentor, he happily embraces that role: representation matters.

Now the assistant principal at a middle school in Texas, the University of Phoenix alumnus makes it clear that he never bemoaned being one of a few black male teachers—in fact, he embraced it. The challenge of "being himself" and not feeling responsible for taking up the podium to speak on behalf of all black male teachers was difficult at first. But he credits it for keeping him in education to help the students who need his perspective.

Roberts' experience is reflected in the voices of many of the NNSTOY fellows we spoke with. They point out that there continue to be consistent and prevalent challenges to diversifying the teaching population within education reform efforts. The paper focused on three primary theories for why black male educators are necessary in the classroom.

- First, black teachers are more likely to be familiar with the cultural needs of black students, thus creating a space for positive academic achievement to occur.
- Second, black male students benefit from having a black male teacher, with *research findings* noting lower dropout rates, fewer disciplinary issues, more positive views of schooling, and better test scores.
- Finally, there is a theory that black educators—with a specific focus on black male educators—have a positive impact on children of all races and the teaching profession as a whole, with *many noting* that the lack of a diversified teacher workforce continues to undermine egalitarianism within society through the reinforcement of persevering social inequalities and inequities.

While schools of thought may vary surrounding the benefits of African American male representation in education, there is an overarching level of agreement: The lack of African American males in teaching positions has serious implications in classroom settings, and diversification needs to be a continuing priority within educational reform efforts. In New York City, Mayor Bill de Blasio's administration launched *NYC Men Teach* in 2015 after data showed that 85 percent of public school students were racial minorities, but 60 percent of those teaching them were white. The question is how effective has their white teacher been in teaching our African American students without knowing the culture of these students?

Why We Need More Black Men in the Classroom

Sundjata Sekou, a third-grade math and science teacher at Mount Vernon Avenue Elementary School in Irvington, shares this with us in the October issue of *NJEA REVIEW.*

Who a student's teacher will be is a lesson in segregation!

If you don't believe me, close your eyes and think about a teacher. Who comes to mind?

More than likely you didn't think of someone who is Black, Latino, Asian, or someone whose lineage is from a predominantly Muslim country. You probably thought of a white person. Being more descriptive, you more than likely thought of a white female. You almost certainly didn't think of someone like me. I am black, male, and a teacher. Yes, we exist in New Jersey! But our numbers are bleak. According to New Jersey Policy Perspective, only 1.7 percent of New Jersey teachers are black males. This issue of black men not being teachers in the classroom affects every student, but it affects black boys disproportionately. When it comes to educational attainment, as a group, black boys are normally at the bottom of most statistical categories. For black boys, this educational crisis starts the moment they are born in a racist American society that applauds their athletic abilities yet shuns their intellectual capabilities.

This educational crisis is exacerbated in K–12 classrooms where most black boys are placed with teachers who may not understand them and cannot relate to them. In turn, the teacher may seem boring to the black male students. To them, the teacher may appear scared of them or agitated by their presence. This atmosphere of bias and educational displeasure turns into situations where black boys are thrust into special education at an alarming rate and exhibit a lack of proficiency in reading and mathematics compared to their white counterparts. They are punished more harshly than any other student group. Faced with these circumstances, many black boys drop out and end up being incarcerated.

Sundjata Sekou's life as a black student

Sundjata Sekou goes on to share.

> I was one of those Black boys who was disillusioned by the educational system. After arriving from Jamaica at the age of 9, I witnessed a New Jersey educational system that neglected and showed outward contempt to Black boys.
>
> This system of education hid the contributions of people of African descent and exalted the contributions of people from European descent. This New Jersey educational system rarely had any Black, Latino, or Asian teachers. Even rarer, was the sight of Black men in the classroom.
>
> Faced with a New Jersey education system that derided Black boys, concealed the historical contributions of our ancestors, and rarely had Black male teachers, we rebelled against the system.
>
> Starting in elementary school, my friends and I disrupted the class, our lessons and the teacher. Instead of seeking a program that would reach us, bring out the best in us, and engage us intellectually, our schools suspended us at an alarming rate. By the time we reached the 10th grade, many of my friends stopped going to school.
>
> Faced with a New Jersey education system that derided Black boys, concealed the historical contributions of our ancestors, and rarely had Black male teachers, we rebelled against the system.

Sundjata Sekou's awakening

When I was in the 11th grade, The Autobiography of Malcolm X: As Told to Alex Haley came into my possession. That book spoke to my existence, to what was going on in my urban community, and to my role as a Black boy transitioning into being a Black man in America.

That book answered the who, what, where, and why of the way things are in America. At the root of it was that America has struggled and has not sufficiently dealt with the legacy of the trans-Atlantic slave trade, slavery, Jim Crow, "separate but equal" and racism. These maladies are in the DNA of America and imbued in every system, including the education system. It is not hyperbolic to write that this book changed my life by answering my questions about America.

Armed with this new invigorating knowledge, I graduated high school, community college, state university, and ultimately earned two graduate degrees. Although I endured the educational system and worked for a nonprofit, I kept thinking about Black boys like Jimmy Drama, P-Andre, Debo, Mike, Andy, Sal, and many of my friends who stopped going to school.

I wondered what would have happened if these brilliant Black boys were given a book that resonated with them, had a teacher who believed in them, or were introduced to a curriculum that expanded their knowledge?

Becoming a teacher

As I shared these thoughts with my wife and people who I worked with, each individual would say, "You should become a teacher." For years, I fought the feeling to become a teacher because of what teachers *didn't* do for my friends. But I constantly had two questions in my mind. The first one was, Should I become a teacher? The second and more important question was, What type of teacher will I be?

I decided to become a teacher and vowed to be the teacher I never had. I also sought out the opportunity to work in an urban community. It was the best professional decision I made in my life. I have taught third and fourth grades, but learning is more than what happens in a classroom. Therefore, with support from the principal of my school, I have organized men in the community to welcome students back on the first day of school. I have organized boys-only assemblies where all the men in the building speak to the boys and equally all the women speak to the girls.

Also, every year, I've arranged for students who get suspended, written up, and are disruptive in class to go with the National Honor Society and Student Council students to the Metropolitan Museum of Art in New York City. There they witness evidence of their historical African and Mesoamerican greatness. In the museum, students get knowledge of who they are, what can be accomplished, and why there are artifacts from their ancestors in the museum. Sundjata Sekou mirrors the same experience as many other African American male teachers and African American male students around the country.

There must be a call to action

1. All school boards of education around the country should hire more African American males as teachers. All students need to see African American males in the classroom. But black boys, in particular, many of whom are withering instead of flourishing in classrooms, need to see African American males in the classroom.
2. Black men should be hired, valued, supported, and invited by your black male teachers to be a part of the school leadership team.

3. Do not simply make your black male teachers the unofficial deans of discipline!
4. The New Jersey Department of Education should make existing laws more robust by recruiting black men to become teachers and supporting those Black men who are teachers.

In my state of New Jersey, Governor Phil Murphy signed S-703 into law in 2019, establishing a pilot program within the Department of Education to recruit disadvantaged or minority men to teach in certain underperforming schools under an alternate-route program. If more governors would follow the lead of Governor Phil Murphy, our nation would see more African American male teachers in and out of the classroom who look like the students they teach. Over half of all public school students in New Jersey are students of color, but the teaching workforce does not reflect this reality. Thus, moving forward, districts should hire people of color and, in particular, more African American males!

Also, the New Jersey Legislature should pass Senate Education Chair Teresa Ruiz's recently introduced bills to diversify the state's teaching profession.

1. Become culturally competent in order to academically motivate black boys. The New Jersey School Performance Report indicates that 83.6 percent of teachers in the state are white. A report from New Jersey Policy Perspective titled "New Jersey's Teacher Workforce, 2019" points out that New Jersey teachers are overwhelmingly white and female.

The report states that white women made up 66 percent of the teacher workforce. Because of residential segregation in New Jersey, a classroom could be the first time that a white female teacher is interacting daily with black boys. To build relationships with black boys, white female teachers should become knowledgeable about different aspects of black culture. They must not disregard the impact of racism on black boys' schooling experiences. They must keep in mind the effect of a lack of resources in their communities and parents' negative interaction with the educational establishment.

2. When teaching black boys, train and educate yourself on how to *check your biases at the door!*

This means to make sure that stereotyping of black boys does not cause lower academic expectations and a refusal to recommend them for gifted and talented programs.
Demographics in New Jersey Public Schools October 2020
Students of color: 57.6%
Teachers of color: 16.4%
Non-Latino Black students: 15.0%
Non-Latinx Black teachers: 6.6%
Male teachers: 22.9%[1]
Source: New Jersey Department of Education

---

[1] According to New Jersey Policy Perspective, only 1.6 percent of all teachers are black men. These finding have to change.

CALL ME MISTER

Call me MISTER is arguably the most well-known and long-standing initiative at South Carolina's Clemson University. Founded nearly twenty years ago, the program grooms black male high school students and teaching assistants for teaching careers, and it has since been expanded to other college campuses nationwide. Similarly, since 2017, the Washington, D.C.–based Branch Alliance for Educator Diversity program has partnered with historically black colleges and universities (HBCUs) to support black education majors.

"HBCUs must play a significant role in preparing black teachers who understand our community," Denise Pearson said, project director for a State Higher Education Executive Officers Association collaboration with four HBCUs, focused on increasing minority male representation in the classroom. "We definitely need to be investing in our schools of education."

Still, many education experts say getting more black men, and men in general, interested in teaching must begin with dismantling the stereotype that it's "woman's work" or merely a low-paying, low-reward career.

"There is always room for improvement, but salaries are rising," Lemuel Watson said, dean of the school of education at Indiana University, who consults for the F2MTC initiative. "According to the American Association of Colleges of Teacher Education, or AACTE, teaching actually pays more than other 'helping professions.' So we have to change that mindset about teaching and salaries; however, they should be paid more for the value of their work."

Rickey Wright, an assistant principal at Columbia High School in Decatur, Georgia, says pay is important, but black men should also consider the power they would possess as teachers.

"To have 30 to 100 students observing your every move, every day, that's a huge blessing," he said. "You really get to help mold them into the people they need to be. That's so important."

Drew Martin, director of the KIPP Cooper Norcross Academy in Camden, New Jersey, said, "Better retention of black male teachers must include providing much-needed support. Black men represent about 13 percent of the teaching workforce at KIPP's 11 New Jersey schools, which is about six times higher than the national average." He attributes much of that success to a Teacher in Residency program at many KIPP schools that pairs a new teacher with a "high-performing" veteran teacher for mentoring.

"It's a complicated issue, and there's no one way to fix it, but we do know that it will not get addressed if it's not treated as a priority," he said. "School districts must send a message from the top that teacher diversity is important."

Frank Lee, a black English language learner instructor at an alternative school in Colorado Springs, Colorado, agrees. He says it is up to members of the black community to step in and sign up to become teachers. It's the only way, he said, to ensure that black children—and all children—receive a quality education.

"Filling that void, that gap, in the teaching field is so crucial," Lee said. "As black men, we have real power to make an impact."

Perhaps King sums it up best:

"Black male teachers matter because our kids matter," he said. "Our kids are brilliant, and we're the ones who are best equipped to pull it out of them."

What do I bring to the table?

"African American male teachers bring benefits to classrooms beyond content knowledge and pedagogy."

This is what a recent study from The Education Trust, a national nonprofit advocacy organization that promotes high academic achievement, claims. And it has data to back it up.

Teachers of color represent only 18 percent of the teaching population in the United States, and black teachers are 7 percent of the teaching population, according to the "Through Our Eyes:

Perspectives and Reflection from Black Teachers," a report published late last year that gives voice to black teachers.

And yet today more than ever, the report rings true throughout America's schools. In the midst of the personal accounts from teachers, the report cites the reasons that continuing to recruit teachers of color, as well as identifying and creating more ways to retain them, is important. It also explains the impact that African American male teachers have on students and the relevance of establishing relationships with students and parents.

The Education Trust promotes high academic achievement for all students at all levels, prekindergarten through college. Its goal is to "close the gaps in opportunity and achievement that consign far too many young people—especially those from low-income families or who is Black, Latino, or American Indian—to lives on the margins of the American mainstream."

> I make sure I get to know each of my students, and let them know that they can do it.

I have experienced what research has shown: As role models, parental figures, and advocates, black male teachers can build relationships with students of color that help those students feel connected to their schools. And they are more likely to be able to enhance cultural understanding among white colleagues, teachers, and students.

Acting as *warm demanders*, they more frequently hold high expectations for all students and use connections with students to establish structured classroom discipline. Furthermore, they are more likely to teach in high-need schools that predominantly serve students of color and low-income students. Black male teachers especially are more likely to stay in schools serving black students.

> I wondered what would have happened if these brilliant Black boys were given a book that resonated with them, had a teacher who believed

in them, or were introduced to a curriculum that expanded their knowledge?

They need to see someone who likes them.

State and district leaders recognize the need to diversify the teacher workforce and are working to recruit more black and Hispanic teachers. And their efforts may be paying off: Research shows that the percentage of teachers of color in the workforce grew at twice the rate of white teachers from 1987 to 2012.

The absence of African American male teachers in American classrooms is an issue that must be addressed over this next decade. Currently, less than two out of every one hundred teachers are African American males. African American male teachers are needed in elementary, middle, and high school classrooms. Our presence in the classroom promotes diversity among the teaching staff and benefits all races of students.

Additionally, students who had at least one black teacher in grades K–3 were about 10 percent more likely to be described by their fourth-grade teachers as "persistent" or kids who "made an effort" and "tried to finish difficult work," the researchers found. These students were also marginally more likely to ask questions and talk about school subjects out of class.

Although enrolling in college effect is a positive outcome, one concern, according to the researchers, is that the main enrollment effect is driven by students choosing community college, where degrees aren't as lucrative as those from four-year colleges. It's also unclear how many of the students from the study who enrolled in college eventually graduated because of incomplete data.

The researchers replicated the findings with similar data for North Carolina students.

"That we find similar patterns in two states—that black students, especially boys, exposed to even one black teacher in elementary school are significantly more likely to graduate high school and aspire to college highlights the pervasiveness of both the underrepresentation of teachers of color and of the importance of role models," coauthor Seth Gershenson said, an associate professor of public administration and policy at American University.

Despite clear benefits for black students from same-race teachers, diversifying the education workforce so that every black student in the United States could have one would mean doubling the current number of black teachers, the researchers say. To put this into context, that would require 8 percent of all black college graduates to become teachers. Given low teacher pay, if that many black college graduates went into education, it would cut roughly one billion dollars from the already languishing cumulative black income.

"For the foreseeable future, black kids are going to go to school and face white female teachers that's the reality, so the question is what are we going to do about that?" Papageorge said, "While we make efforts to find and train new black teachers, we also need to educate white teachers about implicit bias, teach them to be culturally competent, and show them how not to exacerbate these existing achievement gaps."

Regarding teacher expectations, Papageorge and Gershenson previously found that when evaluating the same black student, white teachers expected significantly less academic success than black teachers. Now the researchers show compelling evidence that these biases affect whether students make it to college, graduate, and begin their adult life focused on a career.

Get the Facts

Racial disproportionality in school discipline: Implicit bias Is heavily implicated

Research shows that African American students, and especially African American males, are disciplined more often and receive more out-of-school suspensions and expulsions than white students. Perhaps more alarming is the 2010 finding that over 70 percent of the students involved in school-related arrests or referred to law enforcement were Hispanic or black (Education Week 2013). A 2009–2010 survey of seventy-two thousand schools (kindergarten through high school) shows that while black students made up only 18 percent of those enrolled in the schools sampled, they accounted for 35 percent of those suspended once, 46 percent of those suspended more than once, and 39 percent of all expulsions. Overall, black students were three and a half times more likely to be suspended or expelled than their white peers (Lewin 2012).

The following city-specific data illustrate the magnitude of this problem: African American students in Portland public schools are nearly five times more likely to be expelled or suspended than white students (Cody 2013). According to the *San Francisco Chronicle*, almost 20 percent of Oakland's black male students were suspended at least once in 2011—six times the rate of White students (Lyfe 2012). In Chicago public schools, black students comprised 45 percent of the student body in the 2009–2010 academic year but 76 percent of the suspensions (New York Times, Education 2012).

Data compiled by the Ohio Children's Defense Fund show that the level of disparity between out-of-school suspension rates for black and white students in Ohio's largest urban school districts ranges from a factor of 1.9 to a factor of 13.3. Overall, the disparity factor is 4.0, somewhat higher than the national average. This means that the average black student enrolled in these districts is four times more likely to be suspended than the average white student (Children's Defense Fund, Ohio, 2012).

A 2010 study found that among students who were classified as overtly aggressive, African Americans were more likely to be disciplined than any other group (Horner, Fireman, and Wang 2010). However, this trend varied based on the racial background of the teacher. Researchers have found that once black students and white students are both placed with same-race teachers and are similar on the other covariates, black students' classroom behavior is rated more favorably than white students' behavior (Downey and Pribesh 2004).

Research suggests that Black students as young as age five are routinely suspended and expelled from schools for minor infractions like talking back to teachers or writing on their desks. In a simple analysis of this phenomenon, the overzealous application of "zero-tolerance" policies gets all the blame, but a deeper dig will show a far more complex scenario.

Contrary to the prevailing assumption that African American boys are just getting "what they deserve" when they are disciplined, research shows that these boys do not "act out" in the classroom any more than their white peers. For example, in a study conducted by the Indiana Education Policy Center, researchers conclude the following:

These findings contrast sharply with prevailing stereotypes of African American youth, stereotypes energized by a mental process called "cultural deficit thinking. This process creates the perception that poor African Americans and other marginalized students and their parents as disconnected from the education process.

Consequently, teachers and other school personnel may harbor negative assumptions about the ability, aspirations, and work ethic of these students, especially poor students of color—based on the assumption that they and their families do not value education in the same way it is valued by middle- and upper-income white students. This comment posted on the topix.com blog is emblematic of extreme cultural deficit thinking:

> This perception of disinvestment often creates a stereotype of poor black students as unruly, disruptive and disrespectful. Not surprisingly, research suggests that, generally, African American teachers rate the behavior of African American students more favorable than white teachers.

Implicit bias is heavily implicated as a contributing factor when we analyze the causes of racial disproportionality in school discipline. In this context, implicit bias is defined as the mental process that causes us to have negative feelings and attitudes about people based on characteristics like race, ethnicity, age, and appearance. Because this cognitive process functions in our unconscious mind, we are typically not consciously aware of the negative racial biases that we develop over the course of our lifetime.

In the general population, implicit racial bias often supports the stereotypical caricature of black youth—especially males—as irresponsible, dishonest, and dangerous. In an ideal world, teachers and school administrators would be immune to these unconscious negative attitudes and predispositions about race. But, of course, they are not. So, for example, a 2003 study found that students who displayed a "black walking style" were perceived by their teachers as lower in academic achievement, highly aggressive, and more likely to be in need of special education services (Neal et al. 2003).

At the Kirwan Institute, research suggests that implicit bias is implicated in every aspect of racial and ethnic inequality and injustice. One of the most powerful consequences of implicit racial bias is that it often robs us of a sense of real compassion for and connection to individuals and groups who suffer the burdens of racial inequality and injustice in our society. So, for example, many policy makers and voters feel that people of color who are isolated in segregated low opportunity communities in our major metropolitan areas are just getting "what they deserve." In each of us, implicit bias contributes to the development of an unconscious "hierarchy of caring" that influences who we care about and what groups and individuals are beyond our caring, in a place of invisibility or disposability.

Existing research suggests that implicit racial bias may influence a teacher's expectations for academic success. For example, a 2007 meta-analysis of research found statistically significant evidence that teachers hold lower expectations—either implicitly or explicitly, or both—for African American and Latino children compared to European American children (Rosenthal and Jacobson 1968, Tenenbaum and Ruck 2007). The results of this study align with previous meta-analyses investigating this issue. In a 2002 study, researchers used a sample of 561 elementary school children to determine if a student's race or ethnicity played a role in their susceptibility to teacher "expectancy effects." By conceptualizing teacher expectations as the degree to which teachers over- or underestimated achievement compared to the students' actual academic performance, researchers found that African American children are more likely than white children "to confirm teacher underestimates of ability and less likely to benefit from teacher overestimates of ability" (McKown and Weinstein 2002, p. 176).

Lowered expectations in the classroom may result in differential treatment for students of color, including less praise and more disciplinary action from teachers. Research suggests that when given an opportunity to choose among several disciplinary options for a relatively minor offense, teachers and school administrators often choose more severe punishment for black students than for white students for the same offense. For example, in the 2008–2009 academic year, black students in North Carolina public schools were suspended at rates significantly higher than white students: eight times higher for cell phone use, six times higher for a dress code violation, two times higher for disruptive behavior, and ten times higher for displays of affection (Losen 2010).

When African American male students do *act out* in their classrooms in relatively benign ways, zero-tolerance policies provide the opportunity for teachers and administrators—regardless of race or ethnicity—to apply excessive punishment, not just as a consequence of the minor infraction, but also as a reflection of implicit racial bias and reprisal for the student's perceived cultural deficiency. In California, 48 percent of the 710,000 suspensions issued in the 2011–2012 school year were for "willful defiance," an offense that includes behaviors such as refusing to take off a hat, turn off a cellphone, or failing to wear a school uniform (Los Angeles Times 2013).

During the 2010–2011 school year, according to data from the Ohio Department of Education, only 6 percent of out-of-school suspensions involved weapons or drugs, while 64 percent of suspensions were for disobedient or disruptive behavior, truancy, or intimidation (The Ohio Senate, 2013). Decreasing the rates of incarceration for black men may actually be a matter of improving educational outcomes for black boys in America. In his piece "A Broken Windows Approach to Education Reform," Forbes writer James Marshall Crotty makes a direct connection between dropout and crime rates. He argues that if educators will simply take a highly organized approach to keep kids in school, it will make a difference in the crime statistics of the future.

In Chicago, 75 percent of all students arrested in public schools are African American.

What's most troubling is that not all of the black boys taken from their schools in handcuffs are violent or even criminals. Increasingly, school-assigned law enforcement officers are leading these students from their school hallways for minor offenses, including class disruption, tardiness, and even nonviolent arguments with other students. It seems that it is easier to remove these students from class through the stigma of suspension or arrest than to look for in-school solutions.

School suspension, and certainly arrest, is just the beginning of a life considered on the wrong side of the law for many black boys. By eighteen years of age, 30 percent of black males have been arrested at least once, compared to just 22 percent of white males. Those numbers rise to 49 percent for black men by the age of twenty-three and 38 percent for white males. Researchers from several universities concluded earlier this year that arrests early in life often set the course for more crimes and incarceration throughout the rest of the offender's lifetime.

I have witnessed as a special education teacher the impact of building relationships with parents on the academic improvement of black boys in special ed programs.

In order to change the experience of the hundreds of thousands of black boys in schools across America, we must empower black males to become educators. This is one reason I decided to go back to college after twenty years in the private industry to become a teacher, specifically to be a special education teacher.

CHAPTER 3

METHODOLOGY

The Overview

This chapter describes how the research plan was implemented during the course of study. The demographics are described in detail, and the data collection techniques are discussed, as well as the validity and triangulation and how it relates to my research topic. The chapter ends with a section on the procedures that were implemented during the study of whether or not mentoring helped the inner-city African American male in a positive manner.

Participants/Demographics

The teacher action research was conducted at Grace A. Dunn and Joyce Kilmer Middle Schools, an inner-city public school which is located in Trenton, New Jersey. The school consists of grades six through eight. There are more than nine hundred students of various ethnicities. The socioeconomic status of these students ranges from those living in poverty to lower-middle-class students.

The participants ranged in age from twelve to fourteen years. A total of fifteen students were selected from single-family homes without dads and homes where both parents lived, and students that were in foster care. Only four of the fifteen students were selected for the study. My first study ran from March 2005 to June 2005. Pseudonyms were used to protect the identity of all participants.

Procedures

The teacher action research was conducted over a period of sixteen weeks. The research included several different methods for assessments were used during the research. The various methods of assessment used consisted of student journals, teacher-student interviews, ticket-outs, and rap sessions. These assessments were used throughout the entire sixteen weeks.

Data Collection

Multiple methods of data collection techniques were used throughout the study. The methods used were teacher-student interviews, journal entries, ticket-outs, and group rap sessions. These data collection techniques were used to measure the effectiveness of the study. Using these methods for data collection achieved triangulation. According to Marshall and Rossman (1999), triangulation is "the act of bringing more than one source of data to bear on a single point. Triangulation required designing a study in which multiple cases were used and multiple informants or more than one data gathering technique is used."

Interviews

During the course of the study, teacher-student interviews were conducted. The interview consisted of preinterview questions which were open-ended questions. The interviews were used to build trusting relationships with students and to promote communication.

Student journals

Throughout this course of study and research, students communicated their thoughts about life and what life has brought their way. The students often shared what it is like to not have their dads around and some not knowing who their dads were. The journal entries were used as an aide to help guide the teachers in their quest to help direct the students.

Rap sessions

Throughout the teacher action research project, rap sessions were used to promote group discussion and achieve participation from students and to help build trust and openness throughout the group. Students were given various topics for discussion each session. Students were encouraged to bring topics that they wanted to share. Students were asked to write a journal entry for each session.

Through this method of data collection, we were able to assess the students on their openness to share with the group and to assess their comfort level.

Tickets out

The final data collection technique used was a ticket out. Students were asked to communicate their feelings for the session of the day. Students were encouraged to write a least one paragraph for ticket-outs. This data collection was using gage to better understand the student and to find what was on their minds.

Validity

Glanz (2003) describes validity as "the extent to which a test, survey, or some other instrument measures what it is intended to measure" (p. 64). In other words, it is trustworthy. Since this study was teacher action research, this validity type possesses what is known as internal validity. Teacher action research is qualitative research.

Therefore, the results are only able to be analyzed within the environment in which it took place.

In this teacher action research project, the following methods of internal validity are used: process validity, catalytic validity, dialogic validity, and outcome validity. The results of the research determined what methods of assessment strategies will be used in the remainder of the project. The results from my research were shared with colleagues.

Process validity

Process validity ensures a strong, dependable process that is well planned and carefully implemented (Glanz 2003, p. 64). The teacher action research process involves planning, implementing, data collection, and drawing conclusions from the research. Process validity was created by the multiple data collection techniques, questionnaires, ticket-outs, journals, and teacher-student interviews, thus providing triangulation, which provides process validity.

Catalytic validity

Catalytic validity implies the degree to which the research process has impacted or changed the participants, which includes the researcher (Anderson, Herr, and Nihlen 1994). The research was used to help students to understand the importance of having a positive role model in their life and being able to trust the adults in their lives. In this action process, students were able to express themselves openly. Throughout this process, levels of interest were also affected during the course of study, for both students and teachers.

Dialogic validity

Dialogic validity involves discussion and brainstorming between the researcher and peers, such as teachers, administrators, and parents (Anderson, Herr, and Nihlen 1994). During the course of the teacher action research, I discussed plans with other African

American male teachers and colleagues who have been through the teacher action research process. I met with my cohort group who were conducting teacher action research projects also. These meetings allowed us to share ideas and trouble with other while enjoying the success that had been already obtained.

Outcome validity

Outcome validity guaranteed that the research is not only meaningful for the present, but it is also characterized by an ongoing rethinking of the problem that suggests future action (Anderson, p. 39). The results of the research done to date were shared with colleagues to determine what future assessment strategies will help foster teacher mentoring of African American males.

Limitations

The most difficult part of my project was when Jason, one of the African American males in the study, found out he and his siblings were going to be adopted. Jason was my best student. He communicated well, he was open, and he often shared with others. He was instrumental in coaching the other young men in the group to share. Jason received the news that he was going up for adoption again. His entire world seemed to have fallen apart.

Jason stopped communicating; he became a problem. Jason started getting into fights and missing school. He just did not seem to care anymore. Jason shared that he had been down that road all too many times, and when it seems that things are going to work out for them, everything falls apart. A few days, after our talk, Jason was moved to another foster home.

Summary

The teacher action research study on mentoring African American males was conducted for the last fifteen years which started in 2004. The participants consisted of fifteen students ranging from twelve to fourteen years of age. The data collection techniques used for this project included students' journal entries, group rap sessions, and student-teacher interviews. By using a variety of techniques, triangulation and validity were revealed throughout this research.

"Triangulation refers to multiple research approaches, data source, and data collection procedures and analytic procedures. It is stated that triangulation strengthens the credibility of data collection and analysis as well as findings" (Glanz 2003, p. 40).

Chapter 4 reports the results from the teacher action research. The information that was collected is evaluated and analyzed to identify any problems or successes in regard to the research of the subject matter.

CHAPTER 4

THE RESULTS

Overview

This research study, teacher mentoring African American males, went as planned. It took place at Grace A. Dunn Middle School 2004–2005 and Joyce Kilmer Middle School 2010–2018 in the Trenton Public School District. I conducted the sixteen-week study with fifteen African American male students which consisted of five sixth- and six seventh graders and five eighth-graders during an after-school club titled the Gentlemen's Club. I began the study by sharing with the students what the Gentlemen's Club was about and what we would be doing over the next sixteen weeks to come.

Students were given questionnaires to supply information, which included name, address, phone number, and present grade level. Students were to bring grades for the last three marking periods. Students were asked to bring homework they needed help with to the program the following day. Students were given the rules to remain in the program. Students were also given a journal to keep for the next sixteen weeks.

Specific Findings

As stated in the "Methodology," I used several means of data collection techniques to answer the action research question. The techniques used were student-teacher interviews, student journal entries, ticket-outs, group rap sessions, and teacher observations. The results from these findings are discussed in the following paragraphs.

Student Journals

Students were asked to make an entry in their journal regarding gangs and gang violence and how it has affected their life and their community. Every student responded to the question that was asked of them. Many of the students wrote how many of their friends tried to get them to join a gang in the city. They also wrote that they have witnessed many of the students in the school being attacked by gangs on the way home from school.

One student wrote of his friend being attacked by eight boys. As a result of the attack, Jay lost partial sight in one eye, and his jaw was broken. On the other hand, one wrote that gangs really make no sense. He went on to say, "What are they fighting over?" Bee Bee said, "The killing makes no sense. All it's doing is causing our people more hardship and pain."

Session 1

In this session, the participants discussed the issues of gang involvement such as gang signs and gang colors. Each student shared his feelings related to gangs. I shared the dangers of being with fellow students they knew were gang members.

In this session, I shared with students' information related to gang colors and various signs. During this session, students were asked to share their journal entries.

The following is a sample from one journal entry.

"Once I get home, I am not allowed to go outside because there have been many gang-related shootings on my block, and because my mother fears for my life. My brothers and I are not able to go outside so. We spend a lot of time in the house watching television.

"My cousin is a gang member, and we both attend the same school. I have been seen with him and even though I am not in a gang they think I am because I walk home with him. I have become a target because I have been seen with him he's my blood what do I do?"

Session 2

The topic for this discussion is personal hygiene. In this session, I shared with the students the importance of personal hygiene and coming into manhood. The topic opens many avenues for discussion as it related to the male body. I shared in this discussion the importance of brushing the teeth and changing the underwear. This brought many undesirable sounds from the young men. During this session, I shared how young men are to take care of themselves and the importance of bathing daily. This session was of great interest to the students. They learned how the male body changes over time and what they needed to know about these changes. We also discussed various issues relating to the male anatomy.

Students talked openly and really wanted to know more. The discussion led to the opposite-sex subject, and the students wanted to know if it was all right to engage in sexual activities. I shared with the students my personal life story about the dangers of having sex before they are mentally able to handle it. Students were asked to make journal entries regarding the session's subject matter. Students used ticket-outs at the conclusion of this session.

Session 3

In this session, I discussed the importance of trust and honesty with oneself and with others. I attempted to continue to build a trust relationship with the participants. I shared with students some of my childhood experiences to assure the students that I had experienced some difficult times in our lives, but with the help of others, I can make it. I stressed to students the willingness to reach out and trust someone to be that guide in their life. Students were encouraged to share with their mentors in a one-on-one session. Students were given questions to answer at the conclusion of the session.

Session 4

The teachers and participants met off-site for a day out. At 8:45 a.m., students met their teachers at the school. At 9:00 a.m., we shared breakfast at Town and Country Diner located in Bordentown, New Jersey. At 10:55 a.m., teachers and participants arrived in the city of Philadelphia to tour the African American Museum of Art.

In this session, we shared with the students the history of our forefathers and the struggles of our race. Students were taught about blacks before America. They were taught of the customs of the Africa the Motherland and how it was taught that "it takes a village to raise a child." Our forefathers taught us how important mentoring was hundreds of years before any programs were written. The students discovered the great contributions of Africans and African Americans. These young men discovered that they came from a line of kings and queens and people of purpose.

In this session, they saw the past of their forefathers and how they gave their lives in order that we might live a life far better than society tells us we can. These young men discovered that black history was far more than Martin Luther King Jr.

In this session, the students discovered how their ancestors wanted to read but were not allowed because it was against the law to teach blacks in America. The students each express the importance of knowledge and how important it is to stay in school and strive to succeed.

The students expressed their feelings about slavery and why things happened the way they did for our people. We were able to redirect the thoughts of the participants from negative to positive. The day ended with a brief discussion about their visit to the African American Museum of Art. The final exercise was the tickets-out, and students were given an assignment for the next session on their thoughts of their visit to the museum.

Students were encouraged to share their thoughts in their journals. This allowed students to communicate what they learned during their tour of the museum.

Session 5

In this session of the study, students were involved in a lesson on dining out and setting a table. Students were given instruction on place settings and dining out. What are the proper utensils to use during breakfast, brunch, lunch, and dinner? Students came together to observe how a table was set for various meals of the day.

The students were shown how the table should be set for breakfast. Students were tested on each table setting and the proper way the table should appear at that given mealtime. Students were asked to make journal entries regarding this lesson. Over the next four days, students were asked to set the table for breakfast, brunch, lunch, and dinner. The students were given a test after several days of instructions.

Session 6

The final test came during session six. Students were asked to dress for dinner, which consisted of a sport coat, dress slacks, and dress shoes. Blue jeans and sneakers were not allowed.

At 6:00 p.m., teachers and students were picked up by a limousine and driven to the city of Philadelphia to The Wok Restaurant at the 15th and Walnut Streets for a night out. Students were tested on what they learned in class. Assessments were made by teachers. Students were asked to write reflections for each session they attended for a homework assignment.

Session 7

I shared with the participants the importance of believing in God and themselves and that they can achieve anything in life if they trust God and believe in themselves. Students were asked in this session to share some of their ideas of what and where they wanted to be in the next ten years.

This session was to teach them the importance of setting goals in life. Students were asked to share with the group their thoughts about the program and their teacher mentor.

Teacher Observation

Throughout the course of this study, observations were used the monitor the effectiveness of the study. Several things were noticed. Students in the program seem to be more respectful toward one another and the adults. Students' grades improved, and homework assignments were now beginning to be completed. Students' self-respect increased, and they began to speak positively and view life through a different lens.

Summary of Findings

In my study, I discovered a lot through all the various assessments used: student-teacher interviews, journals, and rap sessions. The driving force behind this study was that the students know that other teachers and I were concerned and cared about them and what was going on in their lives. Students' journal entries were useful in helping us to aid the student. The rap session provided an open forum for them to express their feelings. The ticket-outs were used as a daily guide to what was going on in the minds of the students. The various assessment tools that were used during this research study all proved to be vital in the success of this project.

Chapter 5 explains the meaning of the results of my study. This chapter includes what I learned during the study and how my expectations were met. It also includes changes that had taken place, which were impacted by those changes, and the overall conclusion of the study.

CHAPTER 5

SUMMARY

Overview

Through my investigation research, I came to understand the importance of mentoring African American males. The purpose of this research study was to examine the effect that teacher mentoring has on African American males in an inner-city school. In this chapter, I discuss what I learned from conducting the research study and the impact that teacher mentoring has on African American males.

This chapter will discuss what experts said about the subject, how this research will affect teaching in the future, how it matched expectations, how it compared to what experts said, and how this research will affect my teaching in the future.

My expectations of the study results

At the beginning of this research study, I had mixed feelings about the subject matter. I was unsure if the students would open up and share and allow me to be a part of their private life. When the study was introduced, the students were excited to be part of the project; others were not so sure if they wanted to be a part. Some students were reluctant to talk at the beginning of the project, but as we developed norms and trust, relationships were formed. The students joined in with no problems.

Results in comparison to experts

For this action research project to be successful, I had to capture the trust of the students as one researcher stated, "Children are complex."

I had to remind myself that many of the African American males were growing up without a father or a positive male role model in their lives. I had to become their friend first and gain the trust of each student. Once that was accomplished, then we were all on common ground. Research stated that when a student feels that a teacher is concerned, they perform better (Weinstein 2000). I must agree with the experts.

Researchers stated that the performance of African American males is influenced by social support and encouragement from teachers (Ladson-Billing 1994). I found this fact to be true throughout this research study because the teacher showed interest in the students and what they were doing. The students were willing to actively participate in the activities throughout the entire project. Rap sessions, student journal entries, and tickets-out activities became more than an assignment.

During these sessions, the students were able to express themselves; it became not just a rap session but turned into a father-and-son conversation, sometimes with shed tears. As researchers stated, African American males need the assurance that the teacher or mentor cares. I have found this research study to be informative, encouraging, and enlightening for myself and the students.

The Takeaway from the Research Study

In this research study, I discovered that many of my African American males are in search of someone who can help direct their life in a positive way. These young black males are crying out for help. I unearthed in this research study that when teacher mentoring takes place, a bond is formed between the teacher and the student.

A lifelong impression began to take place in the life and the mind of the student. I discovered during this study that the student wanted so much to please the teacher; they were seeking my approval, causing them to put forth an extra effort.

During this study, students' homework assignments increased from 50 to 98 percent. Student test scores rose overall. Students' attendance at school increased tremendously. Students' failing GPAs rise. Researcher Weinstein stated that teacher expectation suggests that the teachers have a powerful effect on students' performance throughout this project with the students that were selected and others who took part in this research action project. I witnessed a change in the lives of these young men. Throughout the project, I received several letters from parents speaking of the positive impact the project had on their sons.

Validity issues

To ensure the validity of my research, I discussed my study with colleagues and shared my findings. Glanz stated that validity refers to the extent to which a test survey or some other instruments measures (Glanz 2003, p. 64). I used various methods of internal validity during the study using democratic validity.

Using outcome validity encouraged me to share the findings of the research with colleagues. Process validity ensured various techniques, such as students' journals, teacher-student interviews, ticket-outs, and rap sessions, were used in my research study to provide triangulation and reliability.

Dialogic validity involved discussion and brainstorming between researchers and peers (Glanz 2003). Dialogic validity caused collaboration with others working on the action research as well as other teachers in my building and cohort group. During the collaboration, we were able to identify similar problems and share ideas for solutions to the problems.

The collaboration with my peers afforded me other opportunities to view new ideas and chances for ongoing feedback. The collaboration throughout the research project was pertinent for me to stay abreast of ongoing information.

Catalytic validity

Catalytic validity implies the degree to which the research process has impacted or changed the participants (Glanz 2000). Through catalytic validity, I witness the positive changes that took place in the life of each student. This project brought hope to the life of each student. During this study, I witness boys turning toward the roads to become men.

What This Research Means for My Teaching

Conducting this research has given me a new perspective on mentoring and teaching. Throughout this research project, I used various teaching strategies and techniques to help the students. These strategies and techniques made such a positive impact on the lives of these students. I will continue to do teacher mentoring for my students using all the tools that were used in this research, such as ticket-outs, journal entries, and teacher-student interviews. I will continue my research in hopes to find other ways to help aid the black African American males to become an asset to their community and the world. I have no doubt that if teachers and schools were to become more nurturing and supportive of African American males, we could help save more generations of African American males in the inner city.

Summary

The information presented in this book/research project answered my question. The study has shown and proven the effects that teacher mentoring has on black African American males. Unfortunately, not all the students in my study benefited fully. One eighth-grade student living in foster care was relocated during week four of the study. However, students who remained during the duration of the project benefited enormously.

Throughout the study, students were able to visit places that they've never been to. They experienced a social life that many African American males in the inner city could only dream of. The African American males in this study were taught valuable life skills. They all developed a new sense of trust for teachers and adults alike.

In conclusion, much of what I know concerning the plight of African American males did not come from research but from my personal life growing up as an African American male and raising two African American sons of my own, being mentored by two African American teachers and my uncle. I reflect on my childhood and knowing how much it meant to me as a black male having a positive role model to turn to and having them help navigate my path in life. I strongly believe that if my young African American males had more African American male teachers and strong African American men who would mentor them, we could save more generations of young African American males.

> As iron sharpens iron, so one person sharpens another. (Proverbs 27:17)

Staying sharp and sharping others is vital for mentoring

Here are ten practical ways to sharpen people and bring the best out of them:

1. Show genuine care for people.
   "People don't care how much you know until they know how much you care" (John Maxwell).
2. Provide clear expectations. People need to know where they stand at all times, what's good, and what needs improvement.

3. Engage in regular honest conversations.
    Accountability, truth-telling, critical conversations, confronting difficult issues, and being hard on issues and soft on people.
4. Praise in public and correct and private.
    Brag publicly on the positive, but correct people behind closed doors so you don't speak shame and guilt into their future.
5. Discover and develop people's strengths and passions. When you do, you unlock their potential.
6. Build genuine relationships. Conversation creates relationship, and trust is built upon it.
7. Share the credit. Amazing what gets done when no one hogs the credit and how something so simple motivates others.
8. Speak vision and possibility into people. Believe that sees of greatness are in every person on your team; use your influence to build up others.
9. Share leadership. Look for opportunities to stretch and advance others outward; be ambitious for the success of one another.
10. Have fun along the way. Fun, laughter, and humor are the shortest distance between two people.

ACKNOWLEDGMENTS

There are numerous people who have contributed to this project in various capacities, and I am indebted to them for their support and input over the years. First and foremost, this project could never have materialized if it were not for the support and involvement of a number of key individuals in my life. In keeping, I want to first thank God for giving me life, health, and strength to complete the task that was before me.

To my special sons Michael Anthony II and Matthew Kyle, thanks for enduring love and understanding. Special thanks to Rhonda Coe for your support during this research project and to my family of faith Liberated Word Ministries International for your prayers and continuous support. Special thanks to Delores Sellers for your many words of encouragement.

I am forever grateful to Osceola Thomas who encouraged, helped, and guided my hands throughout this project.

To Chantel Wooten and Terrence Crawford, thank you for your assistance in this project. Thank you, Dana Lakins and Keith Jones, for your words of encouragement.

A special thanks to Dr. Ann Marie Senior and Phillip Jackson for your words of encouragement over the years.

ABOUT THE AUTHOR

Dr. Michael A. Coe, M.Ed, D.Div., is a spiritual leader, mentor, conference speaker, author, and public school special education teacher. Michael believes that African American male teacher mentoring in the public school sector, especially in poor communities, is vital for the survival of African American males and males of color. As a special education teacher for twenty-one years, Michael dedicated his life to bringing change to African American males in the inner-city community. He holds an associate in applied science in general business from Mercer County Community College, West Windsor, New Jersey; a bachelor's of science in biblical studies from Cairn University in Langhorne, Pennsylvania; a master's of education from Gratz College Melrose Park, Pennsylvania; and a post master's degree in school administration from The College of New Jersey, Ewing, New Jersey. He holds a doctorate in divinity from Isaiah University, Daytona Beach, Florida. He holds a New Jersey Teacher of the Handicapped Certificate K–12, Supervisor's Certificate, and Principal's Certificate. Michael is a member of the New Jersey Education Association, New Jersey Black Educators, and New Jersey Education Association Members of Color. He is a senior pastor of Liberated Word International Ministries and Hands Reaching Out Community Development Corporation based in Trenton, New Jersey.

Michael resides in Burlington, New Jersey. He is the father of two sons Michael II and Matthew.

To learn more on how to contact Michael and for availability for a special event, book club appearance, or keynote speaker at a function, please contact via email at manthonycoe1@gmail.com or 609-635-1624.

CPSIA information can be obtained
at www.ICGtesting.com
Printed in the USA
BVHW091514190922
647172BV00006B/20